ALL THE MEMORIES THAT REMAIN

*War, Alzheimer's, and the
Search for a Way Home*

E.M. LIDDICK

ISBN: 978-1-960146-10-6 (hard cover)
        978-1-960146-09-0 (soft cover)

Edited by: Tracy Crow

Library of Congress Control Number: 2023900732

Published by Warren Publishing
Charlotte, NC
www.warrenpublishing.net
Printed in the United States

To Dad
and all who knew his love

*To Dad
and all who knew his love*

"… and what is not filled with memories?"
–Rainer Maria Rilke, "Letter to Sidonie Nadherna von Borutin"

Author's Note

A t present, my father is alive. He is breathing. He has a pulse. He has firing neurons and a functioning brain.

My father is also dead.

That's the effect of Alzheimer's.

While my father's body is functioning, that's the best I can say about his current condition. Because who he was—his smile, laughter, love, work ethic, loyalty, focus on his family, memories, anger, regrets, frustrations—is no more.

It's been that way for years. A decade or more, even. A loathsome truth I tucked away until the inertia of life took over and his condition became as unthinking as the air I breathed.

But my involvement in Afghanistan—my participation in administering death—was to be the force that overcame inertia. And when I came back and heard the first ominous whispers of change within me, that ability to breathe without noticing fell away, and I suddenly came face-to-face not only with post-traumatic stress and moral injury but also unresolved grief over the loss of my father.

This is a story with many threads, wrapped around a skein of hope. A hope found in rediscovered letters and exhumed memories. Only, this story is hard to write. Sometimes the words don't come easily, requiring that I drag them from their resting place deep within my mind and shake them into submission. Sometimes the words flow, but in a way only my tortured psyche can understand.

All of the time, writing this is hard. It's an agonizing convalescence of sorts, one where the body heals, but only after repeatedly ripping the staples from a festering wound. My better sense tells me to stop ripping out those staples, to let the wound scab over and heal in its own time. Then again, it was the buried feelings that nearly destroyed me.

And so what you find on the following pages is raw and emotional. Because my father was both. Because post-traumatic stress and moral injury are both. Because real life is both. It seemed only natural, then, for this story to reflect that reality: to suspend you in disarray with the unanswered questions and unresolved feelings, all told through the vulnerability that epitomizes the fingerprint of humanity.

That gamut of emotionality is also why this story is neither chronological nor linear but mimics the indeterminate disorder of memories, grief, trauma, and healing. It crescendos and crashes in the way healing often involves one step forward and ten steps back—bright epiphanies followed by dark declines. And in the way life knocks you sidewise when memories arise spontaneously with a familiar smell or sound; when a simple gesture evokes a startlingly clear remembrance, and that memory tugs your thoughts in a different direction only to end up parallel. You, lucky reader, are not a bystander but my travel companion, to be tugged up, down, and to the side as we sort through the disarrayed memories and meaning unpacked by life and my father's letters.

Those letters are presented in their raw, unpolished form for similar reasons. Editing his words to correct for grammar, spelling, and punctuation felt inauthentic and dishonest, undermining the narrative; using "[sic]" felt pedantic, leaving an inaccurate impression of our relationship. Besides, there's something endearing in those errors, just like his addition of an imaginary *r* when he pronounced "wash" or "Washington."

Aside from my father's letters, I have on occasion changed names and omitted details, namely to preserve others' privacy or prevent disclosure of classified information. Nonetheless, the memories I share

are real. That's not to say these memories aren't affected by the passage of time—they are. But time has a way of pushing the important pieces to the forefront, allowing the unimportant to recede and providing a richness that cuts through the imperfect blurriness.

This is not some attempt at revisionist history, though. While I largely present only positive—though not always pleasant—memories of my father, these choices should not be seen as an attempt to portray him as some modern-day saint. My father was human, with feet of clay. But just as we should judge all humans, we should judge him: according to the whole and not the parts. He was the sum of his virtues and flaws, accomplishments and failures, magnanimity and resentment, love and anger.

Although this is a story about a father and son, war and Alzheimer's, its essence is an attempt to honor this perfectly imperfect man's life, to allow my father to live on long after Alzheimer's steals his last breath, and, selfishly, to ensure I never forget the lessons he taught me—implicitly and explicitly, good and bad, before and since his diagnosis.

My sincerest hope is that this story touches you in some way, making you laugh, cry, and genuinely think about the truly important things in your life.

Hold your loved ones a bit closer. Live in the moment. And love life as best you can.

-E.M. Liddick

1. Three Men

The commander looks to me. "Any issues, Eric?"

It's 2018, in Afghanistan, and I am an attorney for the 75th Ranger Regiment, now pulling duties as the legal advisor to a joint special operations task force conducting counterterrorism operations. Our mission: locate and capture—or kill—terrorists.

My "morning," like so many others, began a few hours earlier, but that means little when day blurs into night, night into day. I had removed my boots and lain down in my uniform on the well-worn twin-size mattress shortly before the last of our teams began their return to base at about 3:00 a.m.

The pager, habitually positioned on a ledge near my head, buzzed obnoxiously around 5:00 a.m., jolting me awake, spiking my heart rate. I reached for it, desperate to reclaim the silence, before swinging my legs off the bed and exhaling an audible groan.

Sleepwalking and squinting, I made my way down the hall to the joint operations center to answer the page. An eerie silence hovered, a hushed silence unlike that normally found in the few hours between an operation and sunrise. Something like concern mixed with fear swept across the operations chief's face as he described the situation: a teammate wounded in action.

With a start, the fog lifted. My brain revved from zero to sixty, rifling through battle drills and searching for potential legal issues:

Where in Afghanistan is this firefight? Are our guys still taking contact? Is the enemy fire coming from any buildings? What authorities apply here? Are there any civilians in the vicinity? Any protected buildings? Should I wake the lawyer at higher headquarters? "Have you notified the commander and 3 [operations officer]?" I asked.

"Yes."

"Just keep me updated," I said, and with sleep still stuck in the corner of my eyes, I trudged back to my room.

The pager buzzed again not more than an hour later. Rinse and repeat. The endless, perdurable tedium of a deployed existence.

This time, however, a flurry of activity had replaced the previous eerie silence. As the commander and operations officer focused intently on an unfolding situation, I walked over to the chief of operations. In a quiet, solemn voice, he broke the news: the teammate, first wounded, now dead.

Knowing this tragedy could beget more, I sent a runner to wake my deputy and paralegal. When they arrived, I explained the situation and assigned tasks, reminding them that though we all justifiably felt anger, we—the small legal team—needed to be the ones who remained unemotional. I tried to exude confidence and certainty, but my face, I fear, betrayed insecurity and anxiety.

Now, roughly four hours after that first buzz, I am staring at an oversized screen. On it are three congregating individuals, two on bicycles, one who appears young—perhaps a boy, but I can't be sure; this voyeuristic observation offers little perspective of the line between adolescence and adulthood. And the commander is waiting. Waiting on my legal opinion as to whether he can legally kill these three humans. I am their judge; the commander, their jury and executioner.

Staring at that oversized screen in the joint operations center, I begin to imagine their lives and the choices that brought them to this existential moment at the edge of a battle that took the life of our teammate. The three individuals stand in a tight cluster on a dusty road in the early-morning heat, wearing T-shirts rimed with dirt and sweat, gesturing back toward the firefight and their battle against the "invaders," perhaps boasting of their exploits and bravery, while the grim reaper swirls, hovers, and stalks from above, waiting for only three words from me: "No legal objection."

The pressure builds as all eyes turn on me. We believe that these three participated in the firefight that claimed the life of our teammate or were, at the very least, sympathetic to the cause, and now the entire operations center waits, wanting and willing to exact justice, to destroy the enemy. I am the sole remaining impediment to a sentence of death.

Legal advisors aren't trained for this. Sure, we receive instruction on the laws of war, role-play hypothetical scenarios, and participate in realistic training exercises. But none of this can replicate the real-world pressures, can approximate the experience of witnessing warheads strike foreheads.

Even after advising on two hundred to three hundred such strikes, each still feels monumental, intimate, like the first time. And this is how it feels—worse even—as the morass of seething anger, hostility, vengeance, and demand for quick judgment mixes with the pressure generated by the magnitude of the question being asked.

This volatile mixture swirls and time collapses, making the seconds feel like hours as forty eyes glare. I'm running on autopilot, the result of too little sleep, too much caffeine. My heart races, screens lining the wall flash, the air fills with an underwater cacophony of ringing phones and static punctuated by intermittent radio chatter and the murmur of disembodied voices and the click of a pocket knife repeatedly, and unnervingly, flicked open and closed, open and closed, open and closed. I can hardly think over the silent din and pounding in my ears.

I turn to the commander. I'm leery. No legal objections, per se. But this isn't clean-cut. Something doesn't feel right about this proposed strike, about the urgent desire to kill. My intuition demands caution, patience, but no one cares about some lawyer's intuition. They only want the law.

I need my own advisor. Someone I trust. Someone who will support me no matter the decision, no matter the outcome.

"Any issues, Eric?" the commander asks.

"No legal objection."

2. The Immovable Force

I'm seated on the espresso-colored leather couch in the living room of our rented home in Georgia. Sweating, out of breath, staring blankly into oblivion just beyond the beige wall. Marcela is asking me something, but I can't hear her; her voice is muffled, as though she's speaking through a wet cloth. It's a lost cause—no, I'm a lost cause. She can't cut through the silent sound of things irreparably changed.

In that moment, I can touch nothingness. I feel no happiness to be home from another deployment to Afghanistan, no rush of endorphins from the run, no joy at the dogs dancing at my feet.

That's untrue. I feel something: a profundity of sadness.

Marcela doesn't know it yet. Nor do I. Or maybe I do. Maybe I know it in the way one can know a nightmare is only a nightmare, even before waking into reality. But life is collapsing around me.

In case you're unsure, that's metaphorical. Though, most days it doesn't feel that way. Most days it feels as though I'm watching—helplessly, hopelessly—as the mortar fails, the towering walls topple, and the leaden rubble of a meticulously constructed life, one built through sacrifice, hard work, and determination, crushes me.

You might think this collapse stems from the experiences of my last tour in Afghanistan as the legal advisor to a joint special operations task force, from the signature wounds of that war: post-traumatic stress and moral injury. And you wouldn't be wrong. Except, maybe there's more. Some antecedent, perhaps consequential, event.

The "more" can be traced back to an event thirteen years earlier. This is when the cracks in the foundation began, or so it seems. Because that's when, in 2008, my father was diagnosed with younger-onset Alzheimer's. He was fifty-nine.

★★★

Dad was the immovable force in my life.

Born in the interlude between the Second World War and the conflagration in Korea, he came of age in a town largish by Pennsylvanian standards, smallish by most. The town, which is situated along the banks of a snaking river and at the confluence of major roads and rails that traverse the giant keystone, found early prominence as a crossroads for travelers moving by road, rail, or canal. Eventually the town lost its utility, its glacial adaptation outpaced by an indifferent modernity.

Like many others throughout the nation, his birthplace remade itself, capitalizing on the industrial capabilities presented by the coal-fired locomotives choking the rural town. Limestone, textiles, and iron and steel, plus the railroad, provided the means of living for thousands of townspeople, like my grandfather and great-grandfather. Eventually these too disappeared, and the town that had once remade itself lacked the creativity and stamina to do so again.

The town and its economy no doubt influenced my father, even if he took no sizeable part. Strong, hardworking men—tired men with dirty hands, filthy clothes, and empty and dented gray metal lunch pails—surrounded him, modeling the venerated Greatest Generation's perspective on right behaviors and virtuous attitudes, societal expectations and gender norms, marriage, emotions, and the American Dream.

I know little of his childhood or upbringing, insignificant details, or so it seemed in the midst of the insignificant happenings of my childhood, gleaned through piecemeal anecdotes remembered and misremembered by grandparents, contradicted or denied by parents, lost in the way a child views life: narrowly, momentarily, and immortally. But by all accounts, my father found love, encouragement, and support in its mid-twentieth century form in his parents and immediate relations, the oily fingerprints of which left invisible residues on my father, and through him, my brother, sister, and me. My father inherited love and compassion from his mother; a strong will, hard countenance, and clownishness from his father; a short-temper from both; and a generosity, tenderness, congeniality, and enthusiasm for the arts from his uncle. All three, and others, fermented his personality, serving as a complementary yin and yang, supplying the visages of drive and determination, sobriety and humor, anger and patience, love and dissatisfaction that made him not humanly perfect but perfectly human.

My father met my mother in high school, though I've never heard the account of how. The scattershot stories bequeathed over the years lead me to believe their relationship involved the passionate, impatient, and impulsive love belonging to teenagers: the sort of love that, though true and real, seems fated, firm, and forever in the way only teenage lovers believe they understand and only through the trappings of marriage come to learn is anything but. Or maybe it was a love born of something like the precociousness expected then, discommended today: marry, settle, work and propagate, die.

Whatever the case, whatever the cause, they married young, not long after graduating high school. My father was twenty, my mother nineteen. Nine months later, love or convention or both gave birth to my brother. Three years later, love or convention or both gave birth to my sister. I would wait another ten years.

In the meantime, father and mother adhered dutifully to their roles. As with my father's childhood and upbringing, third-person stories about his working life supplement my own memories, filling the gaps yet making it hard to separate truth from fiction, reality from exaggeration. Those stories told the tale of various jobs held, sometimes more than one at a time, made busier by extraneous charitable and community activities I can only assume resulted from some complicated merging of gratification, altruism, and what we might call "networking" today.

My mother performed her role too, one of underappreciated homemaker. It comes as no surprise, then, that the gaps in my memory are narrower when it comes to her daily activities, activities in which I willingly and eagerly participated. Like my father, she epitomized the industriousness of her parents and the age, using her artistic abilities to boost our household's total income. And the sights, smells, and sounds of those activities still loom large: the acetate stencils and inky sponge brushes, the wet ratan palm used to re-cane chairs, the metal heddles shaking and clanging after feeding the shuttle and slamming the beater on the loom.

But the jobs they held before I was old enough to know (or rather care) truly didn't matter. The only job that mattered was one for which neither my father nor mother could apply, dependent not on résumés or connections, bestowed not through abilities, skills, or experience, but by birth: Dad, Mom.

The one job I can remember my father holding, though I didn't know it yet, would also be his last. For much of my life, he worked for the same company, a supplier of materials like the stone, gravel, asphalt, and cement used to construct roads and buildings. He was a loyal man, though his decades working for that company was more the loyalty of convenience and simplicity than true devotion and affection, a truth proven each time the company changed names or was bought by some foreign conglomerate, and revealed through his half-joking, xenophobic remarks ("those damn limeys") in the plainly American tradition of coupling bemoaning with inaction.

My father's new—last—job called him Director of Marketing and Sales, a lofty title that amounted to pricing materials and submitting bids on construction contracts. The "marketing" part of his title seemed superfluous, a wordy but meaningless gift in the way titles now obfuscate responsibilities and overinflate egos.

My father began this new position with that old company shortly after I graduated high school. A more flexible, controllable schedule provided an increased ability to visit him during working hours, and for this reason, the memory of this job, unlike most, stands clear.

I would visit him there, in his office, a flimsy wood-paneled room reminiscent of a 1980s-style basement, located in the quarry's shoddy scale house. My father's desk—steel with wood grain laminate, littered with graph paper and sticky notes, perpetually covered in a layer of dust and dirt deposited by the stone-laden dump trucks that drove by around the clock—displayed reminders of the subjects that mattered most to him: photos of his children, his grandchildren, and his wife; his family. On his walls hung framed certificates and plaques, accolades and achievements, memorabilia and mementos. I would often walk in to find him leaning back in his chair, feet propped on the desk, hands clasped behind his head, daydreaming.

Then came 2008.

That year, my father began experiencing difficulty learning a new skill for completing an old task. It had to do with a spreadsheet and a supervisor who wanted data logged in an "easier" way that pushed my aging baby boomer father to a frustration that soon turned to loathing.

By this time, I had left the Marine Corps reserves, graduated law school, and begun working at a large regional law firm. Though I visited him infrequently, we spoke regularly. Each week my father would submit the spreadsheet to his supervisor; each week his supervisor would return criticism. In our weekly conversations, I noticed the heaviness of this new requirement weighing on him; I could hear the frustration and anxiety as it grew with each passing week, each repeated criticism, each recurring failure.

My brother and I attempted to teach him how to use the Excel formulas; so did his best friend, Jimmy. Yet no matter how many times we provided instruction, no matter how many cheat sheets we created, no matter how many times we held his hand through the process, my father seemed unable to retain the lessons, to develop the self-sufficiency necessary to remake himself too.

Any hope for compassion and understanding from his supervisor quickly evaporated. Faced with an unsympathetic and inflexible boss who refused to accept the data in any other format, and fearful of losing his job only a few years removed from retirement, my father resorted to having others do the work for him. This went on for months.

Why is he having so much trouble learning this? I wondered.

I mentioned this in passing during a conversation with my mother. My parents had divorced fifteen years earlier after twenty-four years of marriage and three children, but she knew him better than any other, save my brother. She also happened to be a nurse who had spent the better part of a decade working in nursing homes, surrounded by the aging and dying.

I heard silence on the other end. Then, with a voice soft and small and with what sounded like concern bordering on fear, she suggested the symptoms resembled Alzheimer's. She mentioned two clinical tests often used to screen for cognitive impairment and recommended informally administering those tests to my father. I could feel warm, sour bile rising into my chest.

There's an unsettling thing that happens when I close my mind to a discomforting potential reality or when I refuse to accept an undesirable outcome: I shut down. It is as though I subconsciously flip a switch, turning off all emotional currents and activating dispassionate action. Maybe you do it too.

It's a coping mechanism, certainly, one learned through experience, not intent: instinctively, without notice. In moderation, for brief flickers of time, it serves a useful purpose, allowing continued functioning in place of an emotional implosion, the way one sets aside sorrow to attend to funeral arrangements or how muscle memory overtakes fear when the car begins to slide on black ice. But in excess, when those feelings remain suppressed, it only serves to heat the core, the emotions bubbling unseen below the surface like pressure building in a volcano.

The genealogy of this coping mechanism presumably dates back to some moment in childhood. Operating unknowingly for years, it took some cataclysmic event to bring about discovery, for the volcano to erupt, for me to notice the repercussions of these buried emotions. As it turns out, that event would be Afghanistan in 2018.

Though I didn't discover this switch until after returning from that deployment, I see its presence in response to my father's possible diagnosis. Repression coupled with action as I researched the test my mother mentioned, printed the instructions, and booked a flight to Pennsylvania.

On an otherwise unremarkable afternoon, I asked him to take a test for me. I don't remember telling him the purpose of the test or hinting at the unspeakable "Alzheimer's," instead hiding it all like a pollster uses neutral questions to avoid response biases. Anyway, the purpose didn't need explaining; the room was already filled with a kind of grim awareness.

We sat on opposite sides of the queen-size bed in what had once been my bedroom. Dad sat staring at me uneasily, hands folded and resting on his one bent leg, his aging body sagging. His demeanor reminded me of a child anticipating a parent's chastisement, and for my part, I probably appeared cold, distant.

I read the instructions to the first question slowly, loudly, the way Americans often give directions to nonnative speakers. "I'm going to say three words that I want you to repeat back to me. Try to remember these words because I will ask you about them later."

He nodded.

"Banana, sunrise, chair." After a short pause, "Now, what were the three words, Dad?"

"Banana …" He shifted his weight restlessly as his eyes darted around the room, searching in space for the words that wouldn't come. The silence stretched, before he shook his head. "I can't remember."

One of three points.

Doing my best to hide the rising panic, we moved on to the next question.

"Okay, next I want you to draw a clock. First, write all of the numbers on the clock face."

Dad picked up the mechanical pencil and began plotting the numbers. A twelve, then a one, then a two, each number preceded by determined thought and painstakingly drawn from some vague recollection of a faraway kindergarten lesson. When he finished,

Dad looked up. A slightly wrinkled forehead replaced his familiar frown lines as he awaited the next instruction—or perhaps it was my approval, the roles between father and son reversed. I smiled at him, hoping to bolster his confidence, mitigate his fears.

"Now, I want you to set the hands to ten past eleven."

Dad stared at me, timorously, as if he couldn't comprehend the words. He thought for a moment and looked down at his bent clock face. Putting pencil to paper, he began to draw a line, then stopped. Without lifting the lead tip from the white sheet, he looked to me. In Dad's eyes I saw hope, or something that looked like hope, as if his eyes were saying, "Is this right?" Or maybe his eyes were saying, "Help me, please."

Impatience pulled at me to guide his hand. But I couldn't help him. Dad needed to do this on his own. All I could offer was a nod of encouragement.

Seeing no rescue, he returned to the assignment. And I watched, as this fifty-nine-year-old man who seemed less and less like Dad drew squiggly lines at uneven lengths in choppy movements toward the twelve and three.

One of two points? Zero of two points?

"Okay, Dad. Last question. Earlier I asked you to remember three words. What were the three words I asked you to remember?"

Of the three words, Dad remembered none. My heart felt heavy.

We didn't speak of the overall score and its implied meaning, choosing to avoid the truth neither of us wished to acknowledge. As if by ignoring reality, we could impose fiction on fact, pushing this uninvited future into oblivion. Then again, the results were written on our faces; the epitaph, on our futures.

I spent a few more days in that familiar childhood home with an unfamiliar father before returning to Louisiana, where I sprang into further action rather than engaging in some meaningful introspection or sitting with the emotions accompanying the suspicions now thrust into proof.

After joining the law firm, I had volunteered with a group of generous and compassionate legal professionals who responded to calls for assistance throughout the legal community. Members of this group offered their time and connections to assist those in need. Normally a recipient of those requests, I sent a message to the group, explaining the situation and soliciting the names of Alzheimer's specialists in Pennsylvania who might agree to evaluate my father.

Separately, I consulted with senior attorneys at the firm who practiced health care law, inquiring into the options available for protecting my father's interests, which, at the time, were primarily economic. Those consultations resulted in letters to my father's employer, through that same unsympathetic boss, ultimately demanding that the employer place my father on paid medical leave.

To be sure, these actions served important, immediate needs. Then again, they also provided a welcome distraction from unwelcome realities: that Alzheimer's would slowly wreck my father's brain and that I was powerless to stop it.

Truthfully, what I should have done—what I needed to do—was grieve.

3. Denise Richards

In April 2004, Tulane University Law School welcomed prospective students to campus for a tour and information session. Tulane had offered me admission the previous December. Drawn by the school's reputation in international law circles as well as Louisiana's heralded status as the last bastion of the Napoleonic Code in the United States, and notwithstanding my father's reticence over his youngest son attending school in New Orleans, the visit represented little more than a formality on a predetermined course. Not even the report of nearby gunshots echoing in the guest house courtyard my first night in the city could sound a retreat.

It was one of those April days when New Orleans hangs on the cusp: when the cold, wet winter air blows through the week or two of heavenly spring, leaving behind the warm, molasses air tied so intimately to life in the Deep South. Even so, the pleasant fragrance of white magnolias, fused with romance, hung in the air, sticking to our senses as we ambled alongside mossy green streetcars clacking and popping up and down St. Charles Avenue.

The tour guide eventually brought us to Weinmann Hall, a modern red brick structure colloquially referred to as "Weinmann High" for the high-schoolish drama that invariably surrounds law students. This building, which seemed out of place amid the Romanesque and Renaissance buildings and mature live oaks dotting the campus, would be home for the next three years.

Once inside, our group followed the guide down a long hallway lined on one side with lockers, eager to peek in on a class in session.

And that's when I met her.

She sat cross-legged on a bench outside the classroom. When the commotion caused by the dozen or so overeager prospective students broke the library-like stillness, she looked up with a piercing stare that lingered too long, as if to express an exasperated "Shh!" before returning with a sigh to the open book on her lap.

I noticed her immediately. It wasn't her figure, though I'm sure it was that too, but her face: the full eyebrows, the wavy chestnut hair that fell just below her shoulders, the pertly pointed and slightly upturned nose. And a certain magnetism—a vibe more than anything, observed yet unproven, an attraction nonetheless, drawing me in as a pistil does a bee.

The bench on which she sat backed up against one of the large bay windows opposite the rows of lockers. The windows looked out onto a courtyard, now empty, where students would often congregate in clusters around large bistro tables and where the dean could be seen alternating between caffeine in one hand and nicotine in the other: slurp, drag, slurp, drag, slurp, drag.

I walked over to the adjacent window, begging for a closer look at her while attempting to remain invisible. The morning light breached the panes, lifting the otherwise claustrophobic interior and resting a sunburst on her unfussy hair. The tour guide went on speaking, but the words receded. Sideways glances and gathering courage, sweaty palms and a racing heart obscured anything but her.

I stood there, feigning attention to the tour guide's speech while straining my peripheral vision. With rolled shoulders and face buried in some property or constitutional law or torts textbook—textbooks I had long imagined myself studying—she remained oblivious to the timid young man crowding her edges. Or maybe she hoped that, by ignoring his existence, he would go away.

I, too, was oblivious. Oblivious to her aloof aura. Unable to discern her bespoken desire to be left alone, like a chatty office colleague who misses the subtle hints of shuffling papers and muttered references to deadlines.

Did I say "unable to discern" above? I admit: it's conceivable I simply resolved to ignore her cues—an impulsiveness learned from watching my father all those years.

Summoning his charm and using the sweetest, most confident-sounding voice, I opened my mouth.

"Excuse me. I'm sorry to interrupt, but has anyone ever told you that you look like Denise Richards?"

Against your better judgment, dear reader, I beg you to suspend disbelief. This was not some pick-up line. She really did resemble a young Denise Richards. But yes, reflecting on the first sentence I ever spoke to her still makes me cringe.

Though I didn't know it at the time, this Denise Richards doppelgänger's first language was Spanish. Judging by the look on her face in that moment, my words might as well have been ancient Greek.

She raised her eyes to meet those of her interloper, unsure as to whether she heard the question correctly. "I'm sorry?"

"Has anyone ever told you that you look like Denise Richards?" I repeated, as if the first time asking the question wasn't bad enough.

"Umm … no."

There was no upward intonation in her voice, the sort of inflection that might suggest indecisiveness in the answer or inquisitiveness about the question. Just a curt, definitive statement intended to end any further intrusion.

"What class are you reading for?" I persisted, still oblivious to her disinterest.

She sighed, pushing the edges of her book into her knees. "Property."

"Yuck."

She nodded, raising her eyebrows.

"What are you doing tonight? Interested in grabbing drinks somewhere?"

"No, I need to study for finals."

"Oh, come now! You need to give yourself a break and have some fun!"

She let out an awkward chuckle chased with a half-smile. "I really need to study. Thanks."

I left New Orleans without knowing her name nor her number.

Unbeknownst to either of us, I also left having met my future wife.

★★★

Four months later, I waved goodbye to my father and set off for New Orleans with my brother and his best friend. The eighteen-hour drive took us through West Virginia, Virginia, Tennessee, Alabama, Mississippi, and into Louisiana; through blazing sunshine and driving rain; through Cracker Barrel lunches and a rest-stop nap ruined by a freeloading tick. Ray and Rick stayed a few days to explore New Orleans before driving home.

Law school began a week later. Orientation involved the usual—speeches, receipt of class schedules and reading assignments, introductions to new names and unfamiliar faces—and concluded with a student organization fair. Tables covered in white tablecloths and bearing signs like Federalist Society, Human Rights Club, Alianza, and Black Law Students Association, among others, were arranged throughout the hallways on the first floor.

Walking around Weinmann High with class schedule in hand, reading the signs at tables manned by rising second- and third-year law students, all of whom seemed impossibly older than twenty-three or twenty-four, I felt a mix of excitement and awe.

"New 1L?" asked a man seated behind the Human Rights Club table, using the shorthand for a first-year law student.

"I am."

"I'm Timothy. Welcome to Tulane!"

Unlike the others, Timothy—not "Tim" or "Timmy"—seemed impossibly younger than twenty-three or twenty-four. A portly guy but kind, he had a round baby face and wore narrow, thick-rimmed rectangular glasses perched atop his short, bulbous-tipped nose. He spoke with a dulcet lilt, and his thin lips seemed to curl under, particularly when he smiled, giving him an air of constant skepticism, as if he were evaluating your trustworthiness with every word.

Timothy wore his short brown hair in the style favored by young college conservatives, though Timothy was anything but. We chatted a bit about our respective hometowns and where we attended college. He provided information about Human Rights Watch and Amnesty International, explained public international law courses, identified the best (and worst) professors, and gave advice on first-year classes.

"Today's my birthday, and a friend's throwing me a party. You should come," he said, flashing a smile and using the heel of his hand to brush his hair to the side.

That evening, I knocked on the door of an apartment in the French Quarter. What felt like the entire 2L student body was gathered in a spacious second-floor living room. Punch bowls, finger foods, balloons and streamers, talking and screaming and laughing filled the few empty spaces remaining. Sensory overload.

Needing some fresh air, I walked to an open window looking out onto Royal Street and joined a woman already standing there. We stood next to each other for a few minutes with not a word spoken, watching the drunks stumble along the cobblestone street, before I finally turned my head to look at her.

I did a double take. "I'm sorry, but you look very familiar. Do I know you?"

A Cheshire cat grin formed on her face. She took a sip of wine from a red plastic cup before matter-of-factly connecting the dots. "You told me I look like Denise Richards." My face must have turned red to the roots.

Her name was Marcela—woman pledged to Mars, a portent perhaps—and we spent the next three, four, five hours, until long after night turned to dawn, recreating the world and solving its problems, discussing physics and the Rwandan genocide and everything in between. She was older, both in years and standing, and had a fiery passion. Just my type. And while her approximation to Denise Richards drew me in, her brain, compassion, and love made me stay.

Our relationship expanded and contracted over the following five semesters, a summer working in Sri Lanka, and a semester abroad when Hurricane Katrina struck. It started loosely, somewhere between dating and hanging out, before becoming more serious. Marcela fell first, hard; I came around later. She clung; I pushed away. We took a break; we reconciled. And after several years and some odd months, in what feels like a heartbeat, we were married in a small civil ceremony on a cold, rainy January day.

★★★

Not long thereafter, in what feels like another heartbeat, came my father's diagnosis and with it, that familiar refrain: distractions by way of stirring exploits. It all goes by a single name. Denial.

In 2011, I heeded a renewed call to military service and left the law firm for a position as a military lawyer in the US Army. It was a curious decision given the relative comfort I enjoyed—sharp mentors, a hefty salary, and a comfortable lifestyle—and only a few years removed from making partner. I explained the decision in terms of guilt and duty, the firm's leadership finding one comprehensible, the other unintelligible. There was truth in that explanation, of course: I had missed the opportunity to deploy with the marines early in the twin wars of Iraq and Afghanistan, and the resounding guilt over having not done my duty created a burgeoning sense of inferiority.

All the same, the outward explanation concealed a truth I refused to acknowledge and served only to convince myself, if not others, of the righteousness of my decision. While I did feel guilt, while I was drawn to serve and deploy in order to fulfill my duty, hindsight suggests this decision was, at least in part, a symptom of something larger, some intensifying condition that had long dogged me—a wandering, in search of something. Bear with me; we'll get to that. In the meantime ...

Service took a toll on our adolescent marriage, as it does for so many service members. We moved six times in seven years. Between those moves, I deployed to Haiti and several times to Afghanistan, leaving Marcela to single-handedly manage a household, a career, her loneliness and fear and frustration and heartsickness. We made friends; we lost friends. We traveled away; we traveled apart.

Fast-forward to 2018. I had just come back from another deployment to Afghanistan. But something felt amiss. I didn't feel like myself. I felt wretchedly lost.

Marcela saw it too. Eleven years of marriage will do that.

We had long before begun sleeping in different rooms, a consequence of my light sleep, her restless snoring, and two dogs who asserted fiefdom over a shrinking queen-size bed. So it was shortly after I returned when, following a late-night argument precipitated by my vacant trance and withdrawn behavior, Marcela's crying from a separate bedroom traversed the bare wooden floors, echoed through the restless home, and found its way into my room, coming to rest on the pillow behind my head.

After a fitful night of sleep, I woke to find her email waiting, like an unwanted gift for which one must bear feigned appreciation. The email followed a pattern that emerged over the years, one neither of us fully understood at the time. I would upset her, she would cry; I would withdraw, she would draft her missive. This approach may have minimized conflict in our marriage, all but eliminating bouts of shouting, but it wasn't particularly healthy or productive, and I began to resent these emails just as Marcela did sending them.

I read the email, the details of which, though not the sentiments, have long ago been forgotten. Marcela's message boiled down to an observation and an ultimatum: something was wrong, and we needed to have a serious conversation. The ultimatum assigned a deadline, insisting that the conversation occur sometime in the six days remaining before my scheduled shoulder surgery—a generous, if not coercive, allotment.

As with the details, the memory of the emotions encountered reading her email, and later while stewing on her ultimatum, was buried under its unsparing, dirty weight. I was feeling annoyed, irritated. Or maybe it was shame and fear. Or maybe it was an emotion for which there exists no name. Whatever the word, whatever the emotion, I begrudgingly bowed to her demands. I fired off a reply before leaving for work. We would talk that weekend.

Though the intervening days remain hazy, the way the outfit you wore on the second Tuesday of the third month during a four o'clock meeting gets lost among the quotidian details of routine life, a tension weeping by dint of apprehension and displeasure shown in the absent conversation and autonomous meals, the unacknowledged passing presence and retreat to individual corners, the separate comings and goings and existing while on the clock in a nippy home.

No such haziness surrounds September 16th, however. That date—that conversation—will forever be seared into the collective memory of husband and wife, burned alongside the dated and undated, the anniversaries, birthdays, deaths, homes, pets, and vacations, the experiences acquired over the course of a relationship, not always recollected in precise detail but with enough specificity to jut out from the routine.

On the appointed afternoon in mid-September, on the sacred day of rest, Marcela and I stepped out onto the back porch of our rented home in the fading Georgia summer and staked out our familiar positions in the reclining canvas lounge chairs as the dogs sniffed around the small barren yard. It was an overcast afternoon, pleasant by Georgia standards, but the muddy clouds overhead appeared saturated with pall as the world around us disappeared from view. Sound evaporated—no warbling birds, no chewing lawnmowers, no laughing neighbors, no children playing, no barking dogs—and smell too. Yet the air felt tangible, cramped even, as though we could pluck the nitrogen, oxygen, carbon dioxide, and distress from the imminence suspended between us.

I had spent that Sunday morning collecting thoughts, summoning fortitude, calming nerves. But now I didn't know what to say. And even when I did, I didn't know how.

Leaning forward in the chair, teetering on the edge, my stomach gurgled. I could feel my jaw stiffening and a hot flash spreading then slackening and cooling by half with a glimpse into her eyes. I broke away, redirecting focus on the quivering and numb hands hanging clasped between my legs, before blowing a long breath through pursed lips.

Turning to meet her but gazing past, I began. "I'm not in the right frame of mind to have this conversation," the words bursting forth from muteness in a calm, wispy tone tinged with frustration, "but you've kind of forced my hand."

Marcela listened, her eyes searching, waiting. For someone who enjoyed thinking out loud and speaking in stream of consciousness, she knew when, and how, to not.

And that's when I emptied the contents of my heart onto her in one rambling, incoherent, chunky mess, confessing in vague details things that had happened in Afghanistan and trying to explain that I no longer knew who I was, that I was "really fucked up" from the experience, that I feared I would never be the same person again. "I made an appointment with the regimental psych," I added, words intended to assure her before she even understood she needed assurance.

I was looking down at my hands now but glanced up at Marcela, holding her watery gaze for a few seconds. She rose from her chair and closed the distance, squatting and placing her hands on my knees, searching my eyes as if trying to find something she had lost or a hint of what so far seemed missing. I stared past her at something like extinction. I wasn't done. And I think she knew.

The earth picked up speed. My head started spinning. My stomach churned again. "I love you and I always will," I continued, almost spontaneously, before pausing a pause filled with lingering sadness. I peeked at her eyes—eyes that swam with love—before breaking away again. Another lump formed in my throat.

With tears in my voice, I spewed in sharp truth the final vile phrase. "But I'm not in love with you … and I haven't been for some time."

My body convulsed as a boundless knot, formed over a decade and wound even tighter during the previous week, unraveled, and I purged the repressed emotions, each a cord responsive to the signs of a lapsed honeymoon. Like the ennui that begged for adventure only to meet wary rebuke, or the time spent together yet disconnected, or the deep conversations replaced with ones about shopping lists and bills and chores, or the passionate-turned-perfunctory sex, or the biting of tongues over empty soda cans and open cabinets and dishes left in the sink, or the safety to express thoughts or insecurities eroded by patronizing comments or cold receptions, or the uninspired celebrations of birthdays and anniversaries and holidays, or the isolation sometimes created by military service, or the papering over of a father's medical condition and another father's untimely death— none of which was the fault of either, but just was.

"What do you mean you're not in love with me anymore?" she asked, pulling her hands away, her voice catching on "in love," each word becoming more unintelligible.

Marcela stumbled back to her chair, with hand pressed against her breast in some vain attempt to soothe her aching heart, while at the same time raising her eyes and dropping into her native tongue, pleading "Dios mio" through sobs stifled not by virtue of strength but disbelief.

Time and the space around us seemed distant, almost nonexistent: a dreamlike state, a black hole swallowing reality. Only the snap of a twig reminded me that the dogs were still outside and this wasn't a dream.

"I don't know ..." I looked down at a crack in the cement porch and wiped snot from my nose, the congealed mucus pulling away in one long string bowed by the weight of gravity. "I don't know how to explain it. All I can do is describe how I feel. I can't do more than that because I just don't know. I'm sorry."

Marcela flopped forward, heaving and shaking. A few minutes passed like this. Another snap of a twig to assert reality.

When the heaving and shaking subsided, Marcela lifted the hand from her breast and covered her open mouth, holding the grief within. Staring straight ahead—now it was she who stared into the distance at something like extinction—her wet eyes blinked rapidly until another swell forced her to squeeze them shut.

From a dull ache, some extralinguistic phantom pain, came a chronic need to fill the silence. "I'm really sorry. I know you probably hate me."

Marcela immediately faced me. She wore a grimace, an expression that came off as anger and that suddenly and most violently tore the air from my chest. Her words, though, dispelled the misimpression. "I don't hate you. I hurt badly, yes. But I don't hate you."

Despite the indescribable hurt Marcela felt just then, in that eon inside seconds when I stripped her of the refuge in our love, something remarkable, unexpected though stirring, overcame her. It was the need to love harder. And in that moment Marcela returned to me, her love persevering above all else, cradling me against her chest as I rocked back and forth to the throb of her racing heart against my ear, and we grieved together as one, sobbing until we could sob no more. After all, what more is there to do in the face of such a seismic, world-shattering revelation?

After the retching abated, we did our best to limp through what it all meant for us, for our future. Marcela asked if I wanted a divorce. I expressed only fear, though more was doubtless present: fear of what to do, fear of making the wrong decision, fear of not knowing who I was anymore, fear that I might never be the old me again. I explained that for years it had felt as though we were sleepwalking through our marriage, more roommates and business partners than spouses. I recalled a conversation we had several years earlier about whether I should apply for the position that, although neither of us knew it yet, would take me on that last, fateful deployment; how Marcela warned that if I were selected for that position with the Army Rangers, she did not want a repeat of her experience following my first deployment in 2013 when she had walked on pins and needles, fretting about doing everything perfectly for me, an experience that "set our relationship back five years," she added as a period; and how her period had caught me off guard because it represented the first time she had mentioned any such setback. As the unraveling continued, it became apparent we both had our secretive knots.

The exhausting, heartrending conversation went on for hour after indistinguishable hour as the afternoon stretched into twilight. And while there was much left to say, our voices failed us, trailing off into a dark, hollow, sorry silence.

I met with the unit psychologist the next day.

"So what's going on?" he asked coolly, with the same unassuming open-ended question, or some variation thereof, all therapists inevitably use to uncork new patients.

I walked him through the latest deployment—the death of a unit member shortly after taking over for my predecessor, the pressure campaign following the teammate's death, the longest, heaviest week in August, the panic attacks, the numbness—and couldn't keep it together, the suffering stinging my already-stung eyes. Wearing the patience and sympathy of a priest hearing a soul-baring confession, he listened attentively as I stammered and mumbled and stumbled and wandered and rambled along, voice cracking and pitching higher as I choked back another heave.

With the monologue concluded, he asked a series of questions. I knew what he was doing, why he was asking, though it took a few questions to make the connection. He noticed the distress building on my face with each question, each symptom. After another answer, he stopped. "Do you know why I'm asking you these questions?"

I nodded before looking down at the hands in my lap, noticing for the first time that my right hand had been fussing with the metal memorial bracelet trapping the past around my left wrist. I continued picking at its edges with what remained of a fingernail, the dull ting of the metal filling the uncomfortable silence with each pluck, and waited.

His voice cut in between tings. I raised my head with a final pluck and stared, unblinking, as the unsurprising but still strange words "post-traumatic stress disorder" bore down, my mind spiraling into a galaxy filled with panic and denial.

But those feelings weren't new. No, I had felt them all before. In 2008, with my father's diagnosis.

★★★

This is the state of play—the stakes, you could say. The life I imagined when I left for boot camp, or separated from the Marine Corps reserves, or moved to New Orleans for law school, or married

Marcela, or started at the law firm, or left the firm for the Army, or was selected to serve as an Army Ranger seems unimaginable now. In a span of ten years, from October 2008 to September 2018, I somehow lost my father, my marriage, my career, my identity, and my mind. In other words, my life.

This sounds like the start of a confession. Though why shouldn't it? I have to believe the path to healing, whatever that means, is to find forgiveness, redemption. But redemption cannot exist without confession and repentance. And I need redemption. Otherwise, the sins of Afghanistan will consign me to an agonizing purgatory of eternal remorse. Or worse.

Yet how do I find redemption when I can't even unpack the emotions of all that, all of what's happened in this ten-year span? Because on any given day, I am caught in a tornado of thoughts and emotions I am powerless to slow, a vortex of dust and debris that makes isolating and suspending a single, articulable particle seem impossible. It's as though my mind is a paradox: blank as a freshly washed chalkboard, the product of a subconsciously constructed breaker against grief's terrifying winds, while at the same time swirling so quickly that it feels like one opaque, static mass. All of which makes this confession, this desperate search for redemption, feel a bit like a fool's errand.

It's frightening, this feeling. To feel as though you're losing your mind, losing control of the one thing that makes you human; to feel as though you're going crazy; and, in that moment, to recognize you're utterly powerless to prevent reality from escaping your grasp. And yet this terrifying recognition brings me closer to him, my father, who confronted this very horror as Alzheimer's slowly erased his memories, denuded his thoughts, destroyed his essence, and robbed him of control before mercilessly—mercifully?—rendering him incapable of recognizing its effects.

I've tried to hide the brainsickness behind an outwardly pleasant, congenial mask and workmanlike productivity. I don't want anyone to know there's something wrong. But this façade is showing cracks, cracks through which leaching light exposes the unseen deterioration, and I can no longer keep up the charade.

Unfortunately, the person to whom I would have turned for advice is gone. Breathing, but not living. Unable to provide advice on Afghanistan, or Marcela, or those other moments, major and minor, when habit would have grabbed the phone and dialed Dad.

Alzheimer's did that. Alzheimer's deprived me of Dad.

But did it? What if there's something Alzheimer's couldn't take?

Eight years before my father's diagnosis, I faced the first test of adversity: Marine Corps boot camp. My father, like many others, sent letters—a recruit's only means of communication with the outside world for those thirteen weeks—to lift, motivate, and remind me that he had not forgotten me.

On the morning of graduation in September 2000, I emptied my footlocker, a rectangular wooden box that stored boot polish, socks, and underwear alongside reminders of home for myriad anonymous recruits across the years, and stuffed everything that made me a nobody and a somebody into two olive green seabags, including my father's letters.

Maybe it was haste that led me to toss the letters into these bags rather than a garbage can, as others had in their desire to leave those weeks behind as soon as possible. Maybe it was forgetfulness. Maybe it was an unexplained prescience or universal force guiding my hand. I am certain it was not sentimentality or perpetuity. Regardless, my father's letters made the journey home. There, in an empty shoebox on the top shelf of a dark walnut particleboard wardrobe in the bedroom of my childhood home, his letters remained for years, preserved like artifacts: collecting dust, paper aging and handwriting fading, quiet and forgotten.

I wouldn't think about those letters again until my father's diagnosis.

On a different trip to Pennsylvania, in late 2008, after his diagnosis, I retrieved the neglected box from the same location where it had sat for years. I didn't know what to do with the contents, only that I needed those letters, to collect them for safekeeping.

For the next decade, that shoebox moved from one shelf to another, across the height of the United States, where the letters would remain tucked away, preserved, quiet and forgotten again—waiting for the forces of life to illuminate the words on those pages, to give them some meaning, the way a book that exceeds our experience somehow takes on new meaning later in life.

Faced with all of this loss, I wonder: if I listen closely, pay attention, open my heart, is it possible to hear my father's voice once more through the words on those pages? Guiding, teaching, loving, healing?

I sure hope so. Because I need him now, more than ever.

But let's not get ahead of ourselves. To understand Afghanistan, you first need to understand the lawyer's role in the machinery of death.

4. A Cog in the Machine

The reports began surfacing almost a decade into the Global War on Terror: drone pilots operating from within the safety of the United States were beginning to show signs of post-traumatic stress.

I remember balking, laughing even. How could a drone pilot who worked in an air-conditioned box in Nevada or wherever, a pilot who worked eight or ten or twelve hours before returning home for dinner, a pilot who faced no real physical danger suffer from post-traumatic stress or moral injury? *Absurd.*

Now, almost two decades into that same war and confronting my own grief, I ask: How could I have been so wrong?

Much has been written about the invisible wounds of combat, injuries suffered by infantry soldiers, medics, drone pilots, interrogators, special operators, and even journalists, among others. Their wounds seem easy to comprehend, what with their proximity to the action or direct causal link between the push of a button and manufactured death. But no one speaks about the potential for these wounds to affect others, like lawyers, who find themselves far removed from the physical danger or the direct causal link. Yet I feel these wounds within me.

Sure, I was geographically closer to the action, but psychologically I remained nearer Nevada and those drone pilots. I faced little danger beyond the sporadic and ineffective mortar attacks. I didn't receive or return fire, didn't experience friendly fire, didn't fear improvised explosive devices, and, most importantly, didn't approve the strikes or pull the trigger that took another human life. Instead, I was a mere cog in the machinery of death, advising in relative comfort away from the action, fueled by a steady supply of caffeine, snacks, and adrenaline, providing a cloak of legality to the decision-maker's choice to approve a strike, to pull a trigger—to kill.

Even so, every cog contains some *thing*. And this thing has changed since I returned home. I am different, and the difference is the weight of the guilt I feel. But it is not only the moral weight of how even legal advice kills but also the burden of feeling guilty for feeling guilty. Post-traumatic stress and moral injury are reserved for those warriors who have stared down the barrel at another human and pulled the trigger, not some lawyer chasing frosted blueberry Pop-Tarts with hot coffee. Those warriors' suffering seems somehow legitimate; mine does not.

But post-traumatic stress and moral injury—defined by Syracuse University's Moral Injury Project as "the damage done to one's conscience or moral compass when that person perpetrates, witnesses, or fails to prevent acts that transgress one's own moral beliefs, values, or ethical codes of conduct"—don't work that way. No one possesses a monopoly on suffering. Death is a universal truth without a universal response. Trauma knows no geographic limits, affects each of us uniquely, chooses its victim at random. This is why the *Diagnostic and Statistical Manual of Mental Disorders* recognizes not only "directly experiencing" actual or threatened death or serious injury but also "repeated or extreme exposure to details surrounding" those events, including through "electronic media" so long as the "exposure is work related," as a basis for diagnosis. None of us, not even lawyers, are immune.

My role in Afghanistan as part of the United States' larger efforts, though, seemed benign: to provide legal advice to the task force on the application of international law to military operations in furtherance of our mission. There's much about Afghanistan I cannot publicly share, but I had a room off the operations center and carried a limited-range pager everywhere. Not because of any outsize importance but because every decision the task force made moved us linearly toward a singular end: the defeat—often synonymous with death—of those who terrorized civilians and who also wished us harm. And in this carefully orchestrated dance with death, my role was to ensure the task force operated within legal constraints every step along the way.

Every member of the team experienced the hardships associated with a special operations task force deployment. In this regard, my job was hardly unique. But it was uniquely hard. As the legal advisor, I often felt alone, isolated on what seemed like an island in shark-infested waters. While each member, including the legal advisor, contributed in some way toward accomplishing the mission, some viewed the lawyer—rightly or wrongly—with skepticism or scorn, as an obstructionist outsider. As such, my effectiveness depended on working hard to ingratiate myself, to be seen by teammates as something other than a naysayer, to identify solutions and not just problems. The organization, like all special operations task forces, was an unstoppable train, and the pressure to gain acceptance by bowing unquestionably to its lethal mission and intense human passions could be overwhelming. No one wanted to hear "no." They wanted—no, demanded—that I find a way to say "Yes, you may legally kill." And so I had to decide whether to stand on the tracks or hastily jump aboard.

At the same time, I possessed obligations to something larger. The mission of the Judge Advocate General's Corps is to provide "principled counsel," defined as "professional advice on law and policy grounded in the Army Ethic and enduring respect for the Rule of Law, effectively communicated with appropriate candor and moral courage, that influences informed decisions." Although a part of *this* team, I owed a greater duty to protect the Army, and not any one person, by upholding my solemn oath as an officer and attorney to the Constitution and rule of law in the relentless fight against consequentialism. This required a certain amount of neutrality, dispassion, and detachment that only further isolated me from teammates.

A brilliant officer once cautioned me to provide only legal advice. In the military, we refer to this as "staying in your lane." His caution concerned less professional protectionism of discrete tasks and more the weight accorded words spilling from a lawyer's mouth. Other teammates could express concern about a particular action, and the commander would feel free to disregard those concerns. But those words, when expressed by a lawyer, would suddenly become imbued with some mysterious legal aura that might cause the commander to hesitate, to not follow his intuition. Legal advice can, after all, be a heavy thumb on the scale of decision-making.

One can certainly adopt this narrow view, that a lawyer's job is to advise on the law—nothing more, nothing less. And one would be correct, and not. Because this seemingly limited duty is, in reality, quite expansive.

Baked into principled counsel are the Rules of Professional Conduct for Lawyers. These rules require resolving issues "through the exercise of sensitive professional and moral judgment" and permit advice encompassing moral considerations "relevant to the client's situation."

But principled counsel goes further, folding back on itself to make the permissive prescriptive. The reference to "the Army Ethic" incorporates the Army Values, values like honor and integrity. Honor represents a core principle in the law of armed conflict, providing a safe harbor of legitimacy to our actions in the nation's defense.

No body of law, however, can comprehensively codify all that honor demands. A lawful action represents a necessary, but not sufficient, stop on that unpaved road. So integrity fills the potholes. It requires us to act legally *and* honorably under all circumstances and underpins the mandate to exercise moral courage, to choose the hard right over the easy wrong without concern for personal or professional consequences.

Legal advice, then, represents more than the prescriptive rules outlining right from wrong, lawful from unlawful. It also represents and embodies our nation's collective values, a notion found in the murky distinction between the permissive "may" and the normative "should." "Any legal objections, Eric?" asks both. May I take this strike, and should I take this strike? May I kill, and should I kill? The legal advisor must have the integrity to answer both questions fully and candidly. Because the law is not devoid of morality, even when the lawyer is.

There's a military tradition during which leaders heap unstinting praise—sometimes warranted, often not—upon a departing individual for a "job well done." It's known simply and without fanfare as a "farewell."

My farewell occurred the night before leaving the country. With silent video feeds continuing uninterrupted in the background and the war raging around us, I stood before the assembled group as the commander and operations officer lauded my performance as the legal advisor. Ever uncomfortable receiving praise, which always feels exaggerated even when bestowed sincerely, I shifted anxiously and bowed my head, avoiding eye contact with anyone in the smallish close-knit group.

I remember few details from their respective remarks. But sandwiched somewhere between the compliments and commendations was a comment now cemented in my toxic recurring memory. While characterizing the legal advisor's job as "one of the hardest" in the organization, the operations officer described how the legal advisor, like Atlas bearing his heavenly burden, "shoulders the weight of the world."

There was a lightness to the words as they left his mouth, a gossamer percipience that soon descended and settled under the weight of its heavy profundity. And he was right. I felt weighed down by the ball and chain of pressures and responsibilities, something I had been previously unable to divine.

These unrelenting pressures—accomplishing the mission; protecting our teammates; advancing the nation's interests; providing quick and accurate legal advice; ensuring compliance with and respect for the rule of law; finding a legal, ethical, and moral way to utter "yes"; being seen as a team player; exercising moral courage influenced by innumerable variables including atmospherics, optics, personalities, and differences in rank between me and those I advised—generated the weight seated squarely upon my and so many other legal advisors' shoulders.

I felt these pressures greatest during strikes targeting the enemy and its objects. These strikes represented the bulk of my day-to-day responsibilities. In many instances, they were dynamic, arising spontaneously and providing no real moment for deliberation or second opinions, instead requiring a rapid assessment of the known facts and a split-second application of myriad international legal principles, rules of engagement, and theater-level directives and policies.

While every decision demanded precision, few carried the opportunity for error presented by dynamic strikes. Yet because they ultimately coalesced around life or death, these strikes offered no real margin for error. The pressure to provide advice quickly and accurately was indescribable—the consequences grave and irreversible. Wait too long, and teammates die. Wait too little, and a life may be taken unjustly. Though my answers required seconds, the questions persist forever.

In *Politics*, Aristotle asserted that "the law is reason unaffected by desire." But in the pressure cooker of combat, it's hard to divorce desire from reason. We, the members of the task force, did our best, of course. We remained steadfast, professional. No cheering, no high-fives, no celebrating death like some other units. Just the sober execution of the nation's business.

Yet it's hard to ignore the intoxicating human desire for revenge when you've lost a teammate, to ignore the natural inclination to assume that everyone "out there" is the enemy, waiting to kill teammates as their convoy weaves through a dark foreign countryside, to ignore an opportunity to permanently remove one more terrorist from the equation. And it's equally hard to push back against these desires, to be the voice of reason, to speak truth to power, to ensure the team upholds our values and does the "right" thing. But the legal advisor must, because few others will; or perhaps more accurately, because few others can under these circumstances. Because the legal advisor's words carry some additional weight, some additional authority; because the legal advisor represents the last line in the emotional chain of death, the thin line unemotionally demarcating the "may" and "should." Aristotle understood this well: "For man, when perfected, is the best of animals, but, when separated from law and justice, he is the worst of all[.]"

The best legal advisors provide a brake against the unbridled desires that derail reason, desires like the raw conviction to settle the score when the enemy kills one of your own, and supply the connection to law and justice, to each member's perfected self, by unemotionally upholding the rule of law, ensuring that when we exact justice through an eye for an eye, the first eye is the correct one.

But I wasn't one of the best. Because in the heat of moments like these—and others to come later—I bowed to the demands of anger and affability, to expedience and death, rather than to patience, courage, and humanity.

Sometimes, when the night terrors relent, I wonder whether distance from mortal danger adds gravity to one's moral responsibility. Perhaps when you are not on the ground facing existential danger, your role in taking another human life feels more attenuated. Had I been receiving fire, the decision to kill would have been, in some ways, simpler—no easier and no less serious, but simpler: kill or be killed. But stripped of that human instinct for survival, my role assumed an air of profoundly unjust omnipotence, particularly where my decisions traced forward to the unfortunate, unintended taking of innocent lives.

And that—the meaningless, unnecessary, premature loss of innocent lives—is why living still feels like purgatory.

Many reassure me. "The decisions rested with the commander," they say. "He—not the staff officers, not the machinery, and least of all, not the judge advocate—determined when and where life would be extinguished." If the air of omnipotence surrounded anyone, it surrounded him.

Rationally, I know this to be factually accurate. But factual accuracy is not the mark of moral solvency. Because we fought as a team. The commander's decisions represented the sum of all parts, the accumulation of every effort, every insight, every decision, every analysis, and every action up and down the kill chain. We all partook in that accumulation and its cumulative effect. We all shared in the victories and the mistakes. And any postmortem that attempts to pin an action and its consequences on the commander alone represents little more than a self-serving slippery slope, a foolish sentiment intended to assuage the conscience and avoid individual responsibility. I cannot wash my hands so easily.

Sure, mistakes happen, whether through oversight or impatience or recklessness. The proverbial fog of war, we're told. Yet rationality cannot erase the truth that, sometimes, innocent lives are lost. So I find no comfort in knowing I did my best with the information available at the time. That fiction concerns itself with legal, not moral, responsibility and, as such, cannot offer moral absolution. An action may be legal yet unjust—a decision right yet wrong. And no hollow platitude or legal doctrine or empty "accidents happen" can so easily console or delude the moribund soul of one who participated in an ultimately unjust act.

5. The Way Forward

After driving several hours through idyllic, georgic countryside, I park behind the two-story building that is my father's new nursing home. *His* purgatory. Life's newest unjust act.

It's 2016. Before Afghanistan. Before my life fell apart.

Summers in western Pennsylvania can be muggy, and as I step slowly from the car, the humidity smothers me, making the entire experience all the more insufferable. The nursing home's russet bricks, pitted and rough, bake in the bright afternoon sun, absorbing its radiant warmth. Though the days, months, years pass, the seasons change, the heat replaces the cold, the rain replaces the sun, this place—this counterfeit "home"—remains a perpetually disheartening time capsule of sorrow, a prison of itinerant souls. My resignation turns to frustration as I lazily trod the worn, uneven gray asphalt underfoot, its unclean surface littered with loose pebbles, cigarette butts, wrappers, cracked mud, and grease. I can feel the frustration in my chest, inflamed, scorching my heart.

Several years after my father's diagnosis, sometime around 2013, his condition began to rapidly deteriorate. He began experiencing sundown syndrome, a state of confusion brought about by fading daylight and marked by agitation, aggression, and disorientation. After a few violent outbursts, my brother, stepbrother, stepsister, and I discussed what to do next. The challenges my father's care presented in my stepmother's advanced age had become too much to bear, and because he could not understand or mitigate his actions given the condition, we felt concern for her safety. Since this appeal would be more likely to succeed if pled by her children, my stepbrother and stepsister agreed to take the lead, and not long thereafter, my stepmother agreed to place my father in a nursing home.

Dad quickly made two friends in that home, cavorting and carrying on like teenagers or, worse, inmates running the asylum. One of his favorites, and the individual he followed most closely, was a man with an uncanny resemblance to the late Rodney Dangerfield. Given Dad's passing resemblance to Danny DeVito—a comparison he resisted throughout his life—the two made quite the pair.

Notwithstanding Dad's newfound friends, the aggression and agitation continued. Any hope that medication and around-the-clock care from trained professionals would mollify his temper quickly disappeared. After one-too-many violent outbursts and several involuntary short-term stays in psychiatric units, the nursing home told my stepmother to find another location for his care. Dad had become too much.

The move from that first home to this second one provides the dividing line in my father's Alzheimer's progression. Somewhere between the two, my father stopped talking, ceased to recognize me, and grew increasingly feeble. There would be no more conversing, no more watching my father laugh and cavort with "Rodney" and company, no more watching him show love and affection to the dogs when we brought them in tow to visiting hours. All of this was replaced with sleeping.

And pacing.

Here in this second home, I find Dad at the far end of an interminable hallway. He stands at the opposite window, gazing out at something, at nothing. I stare down the tunnel, my vision blurred at the edges, as the refracted light bathes his sagging body. There is a heaviness to him, as though he's an overgrown sunflower on a spindly stalk, and as he languishes beneath the unbearable weight of this disease, I shrink at the image. Melancholy overtakes me as I begin walking the long, sad fluorescent tunnel, destined to meet him, where, I don't know.

★★★

I knew something in me was off soon after returning home from that last deployment to Afghanistan. It wasn't the panic attacks, though three in approximately twenty-four hours across ten time zones and three airports were worrisome enough. No, the panic attacks were merely harbingers.

It was the running.

Before that final deployment, I had an on-again, off-again relationship with running. The relationship began in high school when I joined the cross-country team. Given my knack for injuries—a broken femur, ankle, radius, and wrist, as well as a concussion, for good measure—and participation in various extracurricular activities—marching band, chorus, musicals, model United Nations, and forensics competitions—cross-country provided an opportunity to be involved in athletics with minimal physical risks while still allowing participation in the artistic and scholastic endeavors my father considered more worthy. I wasn't very good. Not at all, actually. But I stuck with it, largely to earn a letter in athletics, but also because my father refused to allow me to quit anything. After returning from boot camp in the fall following high school graduation, I began training for a marathon, and running soon became a pursuit of pleasure.

As so often happens in relationships, things changed. College, and later law school, offered new distractions and demanded different priorities. Running slowly gave way to studying, working, chasing girls, drinking, and partying. The unintentional hiatus extended from weeks, to months, to years before languishing in laziness and an extra thirty pounds. It was only after graduating from law school and starting at the firm that we reconciled, running and I, and the melting pounds helped to boost my self-esteem.

Over the succeeding years, as I left the law firm and joined the Army and moved from one undesirable location to one slightly less undesirable, running became more and more central to my life, satisfying two innermost needs.

The first was the need for escape. Running provided me with the means for outrunning negative thoughts and reaching that small corner of deeply buried silence away from my inner critic, some transient illusion of peace. The second was the need to test myself.

But just as an addict develops a tolerance and needs a bigger hit to obtain the same high, I needed greater distances to achieve both. So I began running farther and farther to put as much distance between me and the negative thoughts as possible, to spend a little more time in that corner of silence, to restore the equilibrium by physically punishing myself for the things I hated in some perverse form of self-flagellation. Soon ten miles became fifteen; fifteen became twenty.

Every run had a destination, but the journey provided the transcendental escape.

Of course, each increase in distance reset the bar. Testing myself required something more. Some greater challenge. Some greater accomplishment.

That's when I read about ultrarunning. I was seduced by this unfathomable idea of running fifty kilometers, fifty miles, a hundred miles in one unbroken stretch over picturesque mountains, past tranquil lakes, through dense forests, along snaking rivers. Ultrarunning fit perfectly that desire to see how far I could push—to find the mental limit of my human body and then to see how far beyond that line I could go. And each time I found the limit, each time I summoned just enough mental strength to push the edges ever further beyond that self-imposed line, the goalposts moved.

But then something happened. And that something was my hand in the deaths of innocent Afghans. Those deaths changed everything, showing the true breaking point of my mind and spirit. Ultrarunning and everything else had been pretend.

This realization came on slowly at first. Just back from Afghanistan, I would feel a subitaneous urge to sob uncontrollably mid-run, some unknown albatross emerging from the murky mists deep within, the urge becoming so overwhelming that I'd need to slow to a walk to regain my composure.

I was chasing something that was chasing me, but I had nowhere to run. I couldn't outrun the shame, the grief, the pain that had followed me home from that deployment. Each time, I found less and less mental relief from running. Each time, the small corner of deeply buried silence, that illusion of peace, became harder to find. It was as though my lifelong training partner—that inner critic—now ran faster, harder, and longer.

This was the first appearance of a symptom I've come to know well: anhedonia, an inability to find pleasure in the activities once enjoyed. I no longer found pleasure in running because running no longer provided the antidote. Even worse, running now seemed to induce uncontrollable and undesirable emotional responses—the exact responses I sought to outrun. Which is why I lost any desire or motivation to lace up my shoes, step out the door, and take that first tepid leap. Unable to obtain the same release, to locate the same escape, I started shunning running.

Much is made these days of the term "resilience," the ability to face and overcome personal adversity. It's become the buzzword du jour. But in what some might call an over-medicated world, one where charlatans peddle quick fixes over true personal self-improvement, there's something to be said for cultivating the ability to improvise, adapt, and overcome.

Ultrarunning, like many endurance sports, embodies resiliency in practice perhaps better than any other activity. Throughout the duration of an ultramarathon, things will likely go wrong. But even if they don't, your body will fatigue, energy will dip, and "quit" will be the only word between your ears and on your tongue.

Ultrarunners train for these eventualities. In the face of expected and unexpected adversity, ultrarunners improvise. And when all else fails, when nothing seems to work, when the mountains loom large and ultrarunners come face-to-face with their worst moments, many repeat a simple reminder in an attempt to resist the siren call of body and mind to abandon all effort: *relentless forward progress.*

Even when I lacked the desire to run in the past, in the time before Afghanistan, I always seemed able to push past the excuses—to get it over with, to put one foot in front of the other. But after Afghanistan, any excuse, no matter how minor or easily overcome by sheer will, pushed me deeper into the couch.

What held me back? It felt a lot like fear. A fear of the physical pain that naturally accompanies running. The pain felt in the joints and lungs and heart from repetitive pounding and physical exertion. My analysis was correct as to the emotion but mistaken as to the cause. I didn't fear the physical pain associated with running but rather the mental pain that running no longer eliminated or, at the very least, tempered. I feared being unable to outrun the pain. Not the pain in the joints or lungs or heart, but the psychological and psychosomatic pain—the incapacitating grief and sorrow and anger and torment—brought on by memories of those innocent deaths. And, like Pavlov's dog, I became conditioned to the notion that running, rather than the trauma of Afghanistan, was the cause.

This revelation was anything but instantaneous. I recognized the anhedonia almost immediately; the fear of pain later; and the cause later still. But the cause seems largely irrelevant when the effect—the inability to find pleasure in an activity I once enjoyed—remains the same.

In some ways, running had provided an identity. Not in the sense of winning races or setting records, but more in the sense of my reputation—how others viewed me, how running long distances became my calling card. That reputation, however, only added to the pain now evoked by running or not running. Friends and colleagues would ask about plans for future races or how many miles I had logged in any given week. I cringed at every mention of running, concealing with averted eyes and hemming and hawing the crushing weight of shame seated squarely upon my chest, held immobile by self-loathing and unworthiness. The shoulder surgery scheduled for the month following my return in 2018 had provided welcome relief: I could blame the lack of running on "doctor's orders." But such ready-made excuses weren't always available.

There's an interesting philosophical thought experiment known as the Ship of Theseus. While several variations exist, a classic version involves a deteriorating moored ship. As the ship's planks rot, workers replace the planks one by one such that over time, no original planks remain. The fundamental question then becomes one of identity: Is the ship the same? That is, if no old planks remain, is this still the ship of Theseus? Or is this a new ship entirely?

When I index the circumstantial evidence of changes since my return from Afghanistan three years ago, I question whether the former me represents that grand old warship, left moored to an isolated pier on the edge of an endless sea, rotting imperceptibly with the passage of time. Because the new me looks unrecognizable. The emotional and physiological responses—the crying, anger, anxiety, depression; the rapid heart rate, stomach pains, migraines, panic attacks—surprise me, provoked by news reports, innocuous conversations, fear over the future, and flashbacks to the past but also by no identifiable source. A similar current often flows unseen beneath these provocations, the briny water flushing raw wounds created by betrayal, inhumanity, privilege, hypocrisy, dishonesty, immorality, and wickedness. I cannot explain the other distressful moments, like when I am driving on the interstate and imagine, for no obvious reason, being struck by an unannounced missile and finally experiencing from the ground what I watched from above. I sleep poorly most nights, harassed by frequent nightmares, some of which are recurring. Sometimes they feature Afghanistan; other times they speak through metaphors. When the nightmare is particularly vivid, I choose less sleep over more, fearful of slipping back into the alternate universe from which I escaped. I bathe in my own filth of negative thoughts and suffer a perpetual hopelessness. I lack any interest in doing things I once loved, whether it's roasting coffee or running in the mountains, and sometimes a desire for life to end pursues me. I go through bouts of overeating and undereating. My voice breaks and cracks and fades; I can no longer sing. Attention to detail, which I once considered a personal strength, seems nonexistent, as does my short-term memory; I routinely forget basic hygiene. I lack focus, experience difficulty concentrating, and almost every effort seems Herculean. I engage in self-destructive and reckless behavior and can rarely endure a drive without the onset of road rage. I am, on the best of days, emotionally numb, detached, dead. And if that former me—that former identity, splintered and rotted beyond repair—is to be replaced with entirely new planks, what, if anything, of the old me remains? Am *I* still *me*, the ship of Theseus?

★★★

Back in that hallway, Dad turns slowly from the window at the far end and faces me, giving view to his vacant and perplexed stare, his wrinkled brow, his trembling hands. He pauses briefly, nearly motionless, before beginning to shuffle his feet, slowly closing the distance between us.

I stop. He's not walking to me so much as he's walking in my direction. But even this action seems unwitting.

And then Dad stops. Suddenly. Without explanation. There's no obstacle in his path. He just stops, his body seesawing like a boat in a windblown wake. Observing him in this moment, I can, for the first time, see the unseen: his body, committed to walking, being cruelly betrayed by his deteriorating brain. His halt instantiates that deterioration, a glitch in processing, the moment his brain forgets its commands. Beset by an intense, unspeakable anguish, my vision narrows further, my heart sinks.

This seemingly endless moment, which plays out like a scene in a movie, lasts only a few seconds before Dad's brain sparks and sputters, jump-starting his body into motion once more. And once more, I, too, begin reluctantly moving forward to meet him.

We meet in the middle or thereabouts; the location is irrelevant. I look at Dad with a feigned smile, wearing a familiar façade, hoping to read some recognition in his face. But his eyes remain lowered like a shamed child. I stoop, timidly glancing up at the dark brown eyes perched atop wrinkled, darkened skin. In the bags he carries under his eyes, I feel the weight. And in those eyes, I find nothing. If the eyes are windows to the soul, Dad's peer into an infinite black hole. He is lost, and I with him.

Standing upright once more, I turn my body perpendicular to his, allowing him to guide our path. He continues moving in his original direction, continues moving forward, as I slowly, silently walk beside him, hands in pockets, a hangdog expression, and with now-hollow eyes staring mindlessly ahead.

When we reach the far end, Dad stops just short of the window, proof that a remnant of the circuitry linking his eyes and brain remains operational. His hands tremble by his side as he gazes out this window, and I at him. I follow his eyes, attempting to identify the object from the rooftop below at which he directs his attention. With a hand rubbing his back, I speak to him in a hushed tone, foolishly hoping that this time will be different—that on this occasion, Dad will react.

"What do you see, Dad?"

Nothing. No response. No recognition. Disappointment abides.

★★★

This scene would play out again and again with every visit over the succeeding years. I'd count the steps as we shuffled from one end of the second-floor hallway to the other. *One, two, three … one hundred.* Back and forth, back and forth. A cycle knowing no seasons, no bounds, no ends. One foot in front of the other. Sometimes I'd repeat my foolish gamble, asking whether he could see the strung holiday lights or perceive the opalescent fall leaves. Other times, I'd find success moderating any hope for a response, and we'd gaze out the window in silence, lost in a world of two.

More than two years removed from that visit to his second nursing home, and after waking from another nightmare about Afghanistan, I find myself thinking about my father's heavy back-and-forth pacing while lying in bed when I recognize the gentle, muted lilt of rain falling on the brick patio of our temporary Georgia home, whispering to me.

See, I am an unabashed pluviophile. Whether a persistent hanging mist, an incessant daylong drizzle, or a sudden deluge; whether punctuated by thunder or lightning; whether falling straightway or sideways; whether accompanied by cold, clammy air or succeeded by oppressive humidity, I love the rain. I love the majestic cadence, in its varied forms, produced as droplets impinge the many surfaces on their one-way journey from heaven to earth. I love the perfume created as droplets dampen the soil, strike the hot asphalt, cascade from broad leaves, drip from needle ends. I love the way darkness descends to eerily match my innermost mood, leaving only dull, ambient light reflecting in the newly formed puddles. And so, on that morning, fearful of relapsing into the nightmare, I walked outside.

Rain always draws Dad near, conjuring fond memories of the many hours we spent together, sitting on burgundy Adirondack chairs with coffee in hand, its smoky steam curling beneath our noses as we peered into the infinite, attending to the earth's rhythmic pulse. Shielded by our porch's overhang, this became our place of safety. Sometimes we conversed openly, a multifarious mixture of serious and not-so-serious topics. But more often than not, we spoke in the silent interstices, free of all pretense, against the backdrop of the cooling, cleansing water falling from the heavens. Whenever it rained, we could be found sitting there. Close. Together.

Rain became the bridge spanning any distance that separated us. When my dad wrote in a letter early in boot camp, "The other night it was raining and some thunder, lightning. I went out on back porch like we once did. I felt close to you that night as it rained. We will have many chances to do that when you get home. These are the ways I pass time thinking of you. I sit in your room because I feel close to you there," I could feel his love.

Just as I can feel Dad's love while standing on the covered porch of that Georgia home as the rain dances with the memories of Afghanistan and his pacing. *What would Dad say now?*

Leaving the shelter of the overhang, I stand in the cold, steady drizzle with head tilted backward, eyes closed. The water washes over the ridges of my face, mixing with lingering tears, performing its purificatory service, and I can taste my bitter anguish. *How do I move forward, Dad?*

When the bitterness begins to dissolve, I go inside. Soaked and shivering, I peel off the wet clothes, wrap myself in a warm, soft towel, and sit on the edge of the bathtub, staring catatonically at the ivory floor tile, trying to sift through the memories.

With the uncontrollable quivering abated, warm and clothed, I open a computer file containing quotes pulled from my dad's letters to me at boot camp. The rain continues, its rhythm sounding out his words, bringing Dad closer.

"You need to stop questioning and putting the guilt on yourself," he wrote.

But how, Dad? I will never know with certainty whether those three congregating individuals deserved to die. But I will also never unsee, in forever echoing minute detail, the child who sprinted into view from an adjacent courtyard or the crowded marketplace full of children or the slender man as he cradled a child's limp and lifeless body or the frightened family as it sought cover or the woman as she lamented God's indifference. I will never know whether I could have altered fate or prevented the loss of innocent lives had I only done more, only spoken up, only insisted on something—anything—different. This is the punishment for my crimes: the unbearable perdition of what-ifs.

Suddenly, as the dance between the memories of my father's pacing and those of Afghanistan continued, the inertial simplicity and metaphorical lesson of our silent dialogue during the hours of back-and-forth pacing over years of innumerable visits finally hits me. My father paced unconsciously, unwittingly, without destination, but, oddly enough, not unintentionally. He wandered aimlessly, yes, but wandered nonetheless. Forward on a path toward some unknown vision, some unknown end.

The lesson? The way forward—is through. Or, as my dad wrote in another letter, "Keep putting one foot in front of the other." After all, in the face of adversity, sometimes our only option is just that.

And so that's what I intend to do. Relentless forward progress. One step away from the old me and forward on the unclear path to forgiveness, to redemption.

If only I could run.

6. The Longest, Heaviest Week

Sleep comes easily when you double-fist adrenaline and caffeine twenty hours a day for months on end. Eventually the adrenaline wanes, fatigue takes hold, your body reclaims its time. This sleep, though, is anything but restorative. Your body operates in some netherworld, hugging the misty boundary between dreams and reality, deep sleep and consciousness—constantly on edge, tense, anticipating the pinprick that causes you to jump out of your skin.

That edginess never goes away. I can't count the number of times that dreadful pager reminded me of its unwavering presence. It must have numbered in the high three digits. But no matter how many times that pager called, whether I was occupying some netherworld or eating or showering or running a few miles on an aging treadmill, the obnoxious beeping always produced the same response: a contracting tension of the muscles, like a dog awoken by someone stepping on his tail, followed instantaneously, or maybe even simultaneously, by owlish eyes and a full physiological sprint—all before even beginning to register a thought. And so it was on a different morning, in August, about a month after that morning when we lost our teammate and when I felt the mounting pressure to support killing three congregating individuals, two on bicycles, one who appeared young.

I reached for the pager, fumbling in that second of confusion to find the button that would silence the indefatigable vibrating *beep*-beep,

beep-beep, beep-beep. Silence restored, I sighed and wiped the sleep from my eyes, taking a few seconds to reorient myself, feel my body, collect my thoughts before sliding my feet into my boots, pulling the quick-draw laces, and moving toward the door of the cavernous room.

Stepping from the darkness into the light felt otherworldly, as though I had crossed the threshold from a darkened tunnel into the blinding light of day. I shuffled across the swirly cream-colored ceramic tile and past the photocopiers, lowering my eyes to avoid the sting of fluorescent lights reflecting off the whitewashed cinder block walls, unsure if this was a dream or a living nightmare.

The twenty flat-screen televisions lining the front wall provided all the ambient light necessary, giving the joint operations center a tired, mellow glow. I continued shuffling along the five-foot space between the two-tiered rows to the center of the floor. Too tired to talk, I looked to the chief of operations and raised my eyebrows, as if to ask, "What's up?"

He pointed a pen laser at one screen on the wall. I observed the hazy red dot centered on a man silhouetted against a ten-foot mud wall surrounding a two-story home that looked out of place in a country where the population survives on $410 per year.

"Do you see that guy by the wall?"

I did, and I nodded. This is what initiated the pager's beeping and buzzing.

"We've observed him tossing grenades into that compound," He went on, adding additional facts in anticipation of my usual follow-up questions. The process was already old hat.

Except now, the man, illuminated by the crescent moon, only loitered in the darkness.

The silence resumed, interrupted sporadically by the staccato of radio chatter. The chief of operation's situation report carried an unstated question, a question that loomed heavy in the stagnant air. No one needed to speak it, though. I already knew. It was the same question time and again, the question asked hundreds of times, a question I was paid to answer: "Any legal objections to killing this man?" And more often than not, the answer was, "No legal objections."

I kept observing, thinking, temporizing. *What do we know about this man? Where are friendly forces in relation to this home? Who lives there? Who's on shift at my higher headquarters that I can call for a sanity check?*

"I think we need more information, sir," I suggested, looking over at the commander, who had arrived only moments earlier. The commander agreed.

We waited, loitering like the man by the wall.

The siege had begun, though we didn't know that yet. So, too, had the longest, heaviest week of my life.

★★★

On deployments, I always attempted to develop a routine, something controllable that might provide some semblance of normalcy in an otherwise uncontrollable, dynamic environment. Over time, these routines helped tamper anxiety by providing much-needed structure to the days.

What this routine looked like differed with each deployment, a product of changing circumstances, diverse personalities, and individual idiosyncrasies. I tried to always be present, or at least appear present—never being away too long, always arriving before and departing after the commander, parking myself in my seat, toiling. Even so, I needed to break away from my chains at times to exercise, to eat, to shower. That's where the damn pager came into the picture.

Most mornings began with an update to the commander. This update generally lasted an hour, after which most teammates went to grab breakfast. The hour or two immediately following this update often presented the best opportunity for an uninterrupted nap or exercise, but rarely both. If I had managed to eke out more than a few hours of sleep the night before, I might run on the treadmill; if the night had gone long with sleep short, I might opt for a quick nap. Neither afforded immunity from the three-inch-by-two-inch electronic tether.

This morning—the morning when I stared at the loitering man, judging whether I could support his death—I opted to run. After the commander left, I finished scanning my inbox for urgent issues before telling the chief of operations where he could find me.

Two rows of five treadmills lined a mirrored wall. Above the mirrors hung three televisions broadcasting Armed Forces Network. Seasonal sports events and daytime talk shows silently flickered as the closed captions struggled to keep up with the present, a disjointed reality where the words didn't match the action or moving mouths, like some poorly dubbed foreign movie. Choosing a treadmill in the front row, I alternated between staring at the person running toward me and craning my neck to watch some program I couldn't care less about, solely to pass the time.

I gradually increased the speed to a relaxed pace, hoping to pound out five miles before returning to captivity. Tossing the towel over the display to hide the counter slowly ticking upwards a tenth of a mile at a time, I flooded my ears with music and positioned the pager in the small slot at waist level. Anticipating. On edge. Tightly coiled. Waiting on a high state of alert. Unable to fully relax into the run.

Rarely did I finish a run without the pager's interruption. Normally I could expect one interruption, a mid-run break when I would grab everything, sprint across the street, past security, through the cipher-locked doors, up the stairs, down the hall, and into the joint operations center, sweaty and out of breath, ready to absorb, assess, and analyze information before giving advice.

This morning wouldn't be normal.

The first page came before I'd managed to run a mile away. Hit pause on the treadmill, grab my towel, identification badge, and pager, sprint across the street, lock my electronics in the lockbox, present identification, enter the cipher code, sprint up the stairs and down the hall, breathlessly enter the joint operations center, receive a brief from the chief of operations about a developing strike. Absorb. Assess. Analyze. Advise. Watch.

I made it a habit of seeing strikes through to their conclusion. For one, a lot of things could change in the routine of a strike, changes that might require additional legal analysis or advice. More often than not, the routine lacked just that.

The main reason, however, was a belief that my involvement in the kill chain, in the decision to take another human's life, demanded observing the permanent consequences of that participation. Like most, I wished to forget this unfortunate truth. But I needed to remember the seriousness of my role. In many ways, it was about respect—for my humanity and that of the human on the receiving end.

As the dust settled on this strike, and the bright, hot, silverish glow thrown off by pieces of human flesh and blood began to fade, I grabbed my towel and nonchalantly returned to the treadmill. The mid-run break had been long enough to dry the sweat, and the leftover salt caked uncomfortably behind my ears, on my neck. I mounted the treadmill again and pressed start, gently increasing the speed, hoping to finish another four miles uninterrupted, oblivious to the inhuman detachment in it all, to how the abnormal had so easily become normal, infecting but not displacing the routine—a detachment that allowed me to participate in killing another human only to immediately return to the mundanity of the treadmill.

Within a mile came another interruption. Grab my towel, identification badge, and pager, sprint across the street, lock my electronics in the lockbox, present identification, enter the cipher code, sprint up the stairs and down the hall, breathlessly enter the joint operations center, receive a brief from the chief of operations about a developing strike. Absorb. Assess. Analyze. Advise. Watch death come. Grab my towel, return to the treadmill, press start, gently increase the speed. Run. Breathe. Relax. Detach.

Buzz. Beep-beep. Beep-beep. Beep-beep.

Fuck! Sprinting across the road for the third time, I gave up. After advising on whatever was now pulling me away, I would just clean up, put on a uniform, and try again tomorrow.

Upon arriving in the joint operations center, I found all twenty screens focused on a single province. I hit on the abnormality the way one discovers a new building on a street corner after a long absence from town. Each screen revealed a different scene. Groups of heavily armed men in the beds of pickup trucks. Roving bands of heavily armed men ambling down alleyways and busy streets. Heavily armed men loitering, waiting for an opportunity to train their weapons on government forces. Heavily armed men moving in and out of mosques. I needed someone to explain the connection, to help my sleep-deprived brain place the abnormality. And eventually someone did: we were watching a coordinated attack against a provincial capital.

The chief of operations directed me to one screen in particular. Three men stood at the southeast corner of a mud-brick compound, hidden in the shadow cast by the wall in the scorching midmorning sun. The wall surrounded a nondescript home located somewhere in the city. Along the eastern wall ran a dirt alleyway—the same dirt alleyway these men used after allegedly exiting a mosque where we had observed men—*these same men?* I wondered—caching weapons earlier.

This strike belonged to a subordinate task force, though not without our concurrence. We watched as the armed predator stalked, gaining position, awaiting approval to strike. The shadow pulsed as the camera focused, refocused. I sat down on one of the rolling padded benches lining the front edge of the elevated second row in the joint operations center, the balls of my feet barely grazing the floor. My skin itched, tingling as though a yellow sac spider was scampering across my forearm, navigating through the thicket of fine hairs. Ignoring the sensation, I hunched forward, sandwiched both hands under my thighs, and locked in on the screen and bodiless voices of those operating the unmanned aircraft.

This near-catatonic state still feels familiar, even years removed. I imagine it's both symptom and cause: the body's way of distorting past and present, of remembering trauma by reliving the experience. I had spent so many days staring in apathy at the prosaic lives of the characters on the screens, observing their comings and goings, their routines and departures, the activities and happenings that revealed their sameness. Only this intimacy was lost on me: my world, little by little, becoming an unambiguously monochromatic pixilation of potential targets.

Maybe this was the strike that broke through the catatonia. Shortly after the missile began its final path to obliteration, the three men emerged from the shadows and into the sunlit alley. Except now there was a fourth, unidentified man walking a bicycle alongside the other three. He looked to be a teenager. None of us had seen him lurking in the shadows. Even worse, at the same moment, a toddler playing in the adjacent compound's courtyard ran through an exterior door, into the alleyway, and up to the four individuals.

If abject horror has a face, I wore it then. A thousand pounds of cement dropped onto my shoulders as my eyes, or so I imagine, widened in cartoonish slow motion. But this was no cartoon. I opened my mouth; shock swallowed my voice. Stuttering, choking on the words and impending grief, I finally managed to force air through my vocal cords, generating the vibrations that somehow formed the phrase that still haunts my nightmares: "That's a kid!"

Time is a funny thing. Seconds both expand and contract, violating their measures, losing all fixed dimensions—the fabric of life yielding, folding, bending, warping until measured and cut in one defining moment that resets the balance. And so it was as my throat expelled that ghastly phrase, the words emerging with staggering laggardness as a bright flash hurtled through space. I was running a race in which I was handicapped and thousands of steps behind the leader, unable to catch up—the tortoise to the universe's hare, but one where the tortoise never wins. No sooner had the sound of my words dissipated into an air of harsh, unforgiving silence than life was extinguished in the blink of an eye. Five lay dead in the ochre dirt under a bluebird sky.

The floor gave out; the mood turned somber; the air filled with sorrow. Ambient noise grew muffled, distant, like music radiating through the walls of a hopping nightclub. "That was a kid," I repeated over and over, less an exclamation and more disbelief, each increasingly hopeless repetition an attempt to convince myself of the harrowing reality, as though by speaking it aloud, I could somehow unwind the clock and unravel time, reassembling its pieces in an order that resurrected life. My head bowed under the weight and disbelief, my eyes stared at the floor, my brain strained to process what just happened, as if I were momentarily frozen in the razor-thin space between fiction and bleak reality, just on the verge of understanding but not quite there.

Seconds? Minutes? Hours? How long did I sit there, yet nowhere—in denial, heavy, staring at the unappealable sentence of our judgment, the irredeemable injustice of our ways? I'm unsure. But the sensations felt in that space of time, those I remember.

There had been a number of questionable, though not illegal, strikes up to that point. But this felt different. Something snapped. And in the Rorschach test of the darkening patch of earth forming in that alleyway, I saw nothing but a penetrating puncture wound, a hole through which part of me fell away. Something had been taken from me in that moment—naïvete? Hope? Innocence? Yes, the death of innocence, that's what it was—never again to be recovered. A hash mark on the timeline of my life, one severing the before and after, the then and now. I just didn't know it yet.

My tightly coiled body knew, though. I would spend much of the day doubled over, crippled by a deep gnawing in my stomach. A daylong ache oscillating between volatile nausea and piercing pain. A daylong ache that repulsed any hunger. A daylong ache of internal rebellion that went unrecognized, unappreciated, and unheeded.

That internal rebellion persists to this day, spawning the same sour ache anytime something from the past catches up, touches upon the emotions of that week. A constant unwelcome companion. An unbroken string indelibly binding past and present.

Along that unbroken string is a patchwork of images and videos, snippets dangling heavy like wet clothes spaced out at uneven intervals, hung to dry, bowing the line—my memory nothing more than pockets of vivid details floating in a contour-less void where forward and backward, primacy and recency, first and next vanish. I suppose that disorder makes sense: time mutated unpredictably that week, as if it were the bolus blobs of a lava lamp, coming together and separating and shifting in ever-changing, patternless density and tension.

But I digress.

I don't know how long I sat there staring at the screen, but eventually I pushed off the padded bench and walked back to my desk on the opposite side of the floor. Time had been reset. More tasks beckoned. The morning lull swallowed in the eye of a disquieting storm.

Sitting at the desk in a T-shirt and running shorts, I felt a chill course through my body, a shiver funneling from the edges of my shoulders, fanning out through the chest, and moving down into the stomach. Attributing it to my body cooling in the air-conditioned space after the ill-fated run, but frozen and lacking the motivation to shower or put on a uniform, I grabbed a black sweatshirt from my room. After all, given the pace of events this morning, I expected a shower would only be interrupted by another page followed by a wet sprint back across the street. None of that seemed appealing.

As it turned out, my intuition was correct. Strike followed strike followed strike—each one pregnant with twin misfortune and tragedy—as the long morning labored into an even longer afternoon. There were the men carrying weapons, congregating near an idling pickup truck just outside a metal gate that looked like the entrance to an auto body shop. There were the armed men strolling the tree-lined avenue, the canopy obscuring the bystanders peacefully enjoying the day's warmth in the abutting city park. There were the men entering and exiting a mosque, using it to stash weapons among faithful supplicants, blurring the line between the two groups and abusing the protection afforded under international law. When dinnertime arrived impossibly too soon, I had still yet to change out of the T-shirt, shorts, and black sweatshirt into a uniform.

While senior leaders handed responsibility for responding to the siege to the subordinate task force, mine continued, at least initially, to have a hand in approving every strike. And with each request, with each strike, my concerns grew as, little by little, carelessness replaced aggressiveness, recklessness replaced carelessness.

It's hard enough to fight the enemy. It's harder still when you're fighting your own. Like a block of wood in a vise, our task force felt the squeeze from opposing sides. Pressure from above to quell the siege; pressure from below to approve with alacrity the increasingly questionable, dangerous, and reckless strikes so that, in my view, this subordinate task force commander could appease his masters and further his ambitions. When we needed to project a unified effort and focus on the mission—quelling the siege, destroying the enemy— we instead found our focus split, battling the unnecessary political backdooring, power struggles, and pissing contests.

This subordinate commander, maneuvering for more authority, began weaving a convenient narrative that laid blame for any delays or failures in accomplishing the mission at our feet. In a shrewd Machiavellian maneuver accomplished with surprisingly cunning aplomb, he bypassed my commander, going straight to the general overseeing both task forces and alleging that we were slow-rolling approval of his strikes.

The commander pulled me and the operations officer into his office. With an air of bemused disbelief, he pointed to an email and watched as we read the missive. The email, from this subordinate commander direct to the general, told of the former's frustration with our delays, claiming that our task force took more than an hour to approve a strike earlier that day and, as such, endangered partner forces on the ground. Our operations officer, however, had just so happened to time the process, somehow sagely predicting this subordinate commander's next move. Our approval had taken no more than twelve minutes, and only that long because the subordinate task force seemed inept at providing accurate information. Never mind the inconvenient fact that no partner forces had been positioned nearby.

The outright falsehoods and political maneuvering both floored me and sent me through the roof. While the operations officer, who was always magnitudes better at remaining unflappable, betrayed no emotion reading the email, I felt a spontaneous heat boiling to the surface of my skin, almost without notice, until I could no longer control the rage. As an endless stream of expletives let loose, the commander sat in surprised admiration, the corners of his mouth slowly raising in an approving smirk, as though my tirade expressed our collective disbelief, resentment, and outrage. Though my anger was reasonable, in retrospect, I'm not sure why I felt something akin to surprise. Sure, the email and internal lies provided a window into this subordinate commander's character, but I had already gotten a glimpse through the angled blinds.

It's assumed, expected even, that a lawyer will express concern with a strike at some point. Lawyers generally, though not always, possess a risk tolerance lying somewhere below seasoned commanders, who accumulate rank and status by aggressively seizing the initiative and accepting risk. But when a commander and operations officer begin expressing misgivings, the dynamic shifts in an undesirably validating way, generating a sensation that can be mistaken for panic. And so it was that, over the preceding days, the three of us metabolized, in our own way and according to asynchronous timetables, our growing discord with this subordinate commander's recklessness—his utter disregard for standard procedures designed to minimize risks to the mission and innocent civilians.

The commander asked whether he should informally mentor the subordinate commander in an effort to rein him in, stem the tide. The operations officer and I agreed that a superior voicing concern might mitigate future risks to innocent civilians and strategic efforts from an overzealous, reckless commander. We also agreed to engage our counterparts at the subordinate task force, mounting a three-pronged effort to restore patience, safeguards, and professionalism.

Unfortunately, the die had been cast. In response to the email, the general met with the two commanders behind closed doors and bestowed greater autonomy on this subordinate commander. Whether the general was giving this subordinate commander the rope necessary to hang himself or agreed with this subordinate commander's approach is unclear. But his decision left our task force impotent.

It was a recipe for disaster, passed down to a callous chef. Unsurprisingly, the resulting meal was unpalatable. Nothing abated. Feigned caution, patience, and deference quickly gave way to increased riskiness, rashness, and defiance. The situation naturally worsened.

My nightmares routinely feature the reels created during this week, a haunting dreamscape flickering frame by frame. But no reel features more prominently than the one that follows. I can still see every painstaking detail, an unfortunate incongruity when so many other details remain obscured by the clouds filling the ridges and valleys of my brain. I remember. And that, in and of itself, is the conundrum. When I wish to forget, I can only remember; when I wish to remember, I can only forget. An ever-present malady where the dead never die.

The reel begins shortly before impact. A motorcycle races past beige mud-brick buildings along an unpaved road and approaches a single tree growing kitty-corner from the intersection to a dirt alleyway just past a multifamily home. Like God, I can see the future.

In the blink of an eye, death arrives.

My view of the scene orbits past the tree's shadow before drifting and hovering above the small alleyway running parallel to the multifamily home. From this vantage, I can see the point of impact. But where I expect to see one body, there lay two, their dark clothes in stark relief against the settling sienna dust.

I watch a slender old man run into the main thoroughfare. He stoops down, cradling the limp and lifeless body in his arms, his right arm supporting just behind the knees and his left arm, the neck. The body's head bobbles; the legs, clad in dark pants and white tennis shoes, dangle. The old man strains beneath the weight of death and grief, moving the body approximately 100 yards down the alley, the body juxtaposed against the man's frame revealing the horrifying reality. The limp, lifeless body of a child. Another fucking child.

The man kneels, delicately laying the body on the ground. But time affords him no opportunity to process, no private moment to collect his thoughts. Because at the moment he woefully surrenders the body's weight to the earth once more, a woman emerges from a multifamily home, startling him.

The rotund woman frantically sprints, arms and legs flailing, toward the body. The old man summons the strength of protector, blocking her path and forcefully turning her away. She attempts to evade him only to be turned back once more. He's yelling at her to return to their home's sanctuary, its ignorance. But his angry demand falls on deaf ears. She cannot hear him through her inconsolable grief.

She falls to her knees and begins prostrating—her body trembling, her voice begging a merciless God for mercy—before throwing her arms wide, tilting her head back toward the all-seeing eye as a blood-curdling, piercing wail heaves forth from the depths of her heart and leaves her suffocating. In the silent video, I hear her lamentations.

The nightmare often ends there. Except it doesn't. Most days when I close my eyes, I can still read her plaintive expression, hear her howls. Just as raw as the day their—our—lives changed forever. I feel both stabbing my heart as darkness grips my soul. I didn't know their names, but I knew well their grief. And in a thousand lifetimes, I could never become blind to that pain or deaf to those cries.

Or the anger.

★★★

We all make mistakes. Large and small, significant and insignificant. An indelible experience. And these mistakes carry consequences, often mirroring in severity the nature of the mistake.

In boot camp, our drill instructors attempted, in their own way, to impart this lesson upon the nation's youth. Because, like the crack of lead rounds tearing through the fabric of space, mistakes can kill. Unexpectedly—without warning, without prejudice, without distinction.

Their chosen method for imparting this lesson was collective punishment. One recruit fails to execute a perfect right shoulder arms maneuver, everyone suffers. One recruit fails to tighten the bedsheets to form a perfect hospital corner, everyone suffers. One recruit fails to return to his spot on the black line running the length of the squad bay, everyone suffers. One recruit fails to stay awake on fire watch, everyone suffers. One recruit fails to shine his boots or press his uniform or drink water or march in step or organize his footlocker correctly or report correctly or salute correctly or eat correctly or speak correctly, everyone suffers. Because one mistake in the crucible of combat can mean the difference between living and dying. It's a stark awakening, this group accountability.

The drill instructors developed ingenuous forms of punishment. Some of it familiar, such as "the pit": a platoon-sized sandbox where we performed endless repetitions of up-downs, push-ups, sit-ups, mountain climbers, jumping jacks, flutter kicks, and anything else our sadistic masters in Smokey Bear hats dreamed up, only to emerge from the heat of the high, prickly, South Carolina sun looking like sugar cookies from an oven. And some of it unfamiliar, such as rifle maneuvers performed using a twin-size mattress after a bulldog of a drill instructor caught a recruit asleep on fire watch. "Oh, you want to play games?" they'd rhetorically ask the ninety scared-shitless recruits. "Because I've got more games than Milton Bradley."

They could only punish us for so long, their exercises bounded by length and repetition, constrained to marked periods during the training day. Seemingly not even our godlike masters—the very ones who determined the key interrogatives surrounding eating, sleeping, drinking, dressing, showering, shaving, urinating, defecating, reading, writing, speaking, and every other basic human action—were above the law.

We didn't know this, of course. We lived without refuge on the edge of fear every second of every minute of every hour of every day. Instructive fear. Fear designed to teach the body to instinctively remember that mistakes cause pain, kill.

From that fear came stress, and from stress, anger. And a second comprehensive lesson: Our measure was defined by our weakest teammate. Overcoming that weakness required teamwork, not anger, the second being antithetical to a desirable outcome. A lesson learned easily in theory, harder in practice.

Anger, spite, and frustration—it all surfaced quickly when a recruit did or failed to do something that drew the unwanted attention of a drill instructor. Eye-rolling, shouting, and berating preceded the drill instructor's game of the day. Each of us endeavored to avoid being the individual who made the mistake—or, more accurately, got caught making the mistake—that would bring suffering upon the entire platoon.

Leafing through my father's letters, scanning his words, revived these misplaced memories, transporting me back to that summer in 2000 and the platoon's time spent "playing" in that sandbox. Given his responses, I must have written to my father about one recruit in particular, a recruit who generously took it upon himself to ensure our drill instructors never deprived the platoon of adequate "playtime."

Even nearly twenty years later, I can still remember this recruit's gravelly, whiny voice; his wide, unblinking eyes; his anxiety-induced stutter; and his name, which fittingly included "sand," as if he were predestined for the role of platoon villain. I can still hear the drill instructor punishing him with calisthenics on the quarterdeck, sounding out the exercise cadence—"one, two, three"—in his trademark strangulated "frog voice"; how the pain crippled that recruit's voice as he finished off the cadence by screaming the number of repetitions hitherto completed; how that recruit's voice seemed to carry some unambiguous plea for mercy.

No matter how hard he tried, this recruit never seemed capable of meeting our drill instructors' exacting standards. A perpetual fuck-up. More than likely, the drill instructors targeted him, but fear and stress and pain have a certain way of obscuring facts, muddying truth.

My complaints about this recruit and the collective punishment we suffered came early, within weeks of starting boot camp. I may have described his mistakes in great detail in a single letter or mentioned them over the course of several. I can't remember. But at some point, my vociferous griping prompted Dad's impatient written response, seizing upon the word I used to describe this recruit: "Get used to dealing with morons! You will have them throughout your life just not in the service."

The effect of his words was matched by their brevity. No sooner had I read the words meant to pacify than the drill instructors announced lights-out, a new day began, and a fresh source of ire arose. And with it, the foam from the simmering anger spilled over the rim anew, scalding the source and leaving behind scorched white streaks of rolling eyes and shouting and berating.

This "moron" just couldn't learn. Mistakes kill, after all.

★★★

We often believe we know how we'll respond in consequential moments. We imagine those moments, working through the ifs and thens, outlining various plans of action before boldly proclaiming what we'd do in the precise moment when it truly matters, convincing people of our sincerity through forced bravado and repetition.

Except we don't know. It's easy to say *I'd fight back* when removed from the danger of an active shooter; to say *I'd intervene* when removed from the father physically abusing a child in public; to say *I'd leave* when removed from the romantic partner's battery. It's harder to *do*. Because our animal instincts get the deciding vote. Fight or flight or the oft-forgotten freeze—that familiar trilogy of trauma—remain indifferent to our preplanned responses, our hollow words, our supposed honor, our purported values. Sometimes we act as we had claimed we would; sometimes we don't; sometimes we surprise ourselves. But the truth is that notwithstanding our repeated, strenuous assertions to the contrary, we just don't know how we will respond. Until we do.

I thought I knew how I'd respond to actions I considered wrong, if not legally, then morally. Faced with the hard choice, I would fight. I would summon the courage to speak, to act, to intervene, to make it—whatever *it* was—stop.

Don't get me wrong, I tried. I spoke with the commander and operations officer several times about concerns surrounding the risks to innocent civilians created by the strikes during that longest, heaviest week. I asked the subordinate commander's attorney to do something—anything—to get this man to exercise some caution. I voiced my concerns to the senior attorney at our higher headquarters, begging him to recommend an investigation into this subordinate commander's actions. I ranted in the joint operations center and to peers at our higher headquarters. I exploded into a diatribe, my spittle laced with vitriol, about how the subordinate commander "should fucking be relieved of command!"

The absence of action is still action. And when nothing happened, it seemed like no one gave a damn, content instead to sweep the unsightly dirt of war under a carpet: out of sight and out of mind, overlooked, forgotten. But forgotten by whom? Us? The parents of the innocent children he—we—killed?

I tortured myself, clawing at the gray matter, searching for the "next step" on some fictional checklist. *What more can I do? Who can I contact next? What are the consequences of that action?* The torture was no use, though. Nothing I tried made any difference.

Why is no one else upset? I began to question whether I was losing my mind, as though I was suffering from hallucinations and delusions, unable to understand why my apoplectic words weren't causing others to fidget. *Am I completely off base here? Am I missing something that everyone else can see?* Their apparent unconcern left me feeling helpless, screaming for help in a thick, dark forest as the vast expanse swallowed my unechoing voice, leaving me hoarse, abandoned, and alone.

But this illusion about an illusion was also an illusion. I wasn't going crazy. Others in the task force felt the same restiveness, anger, and frustration. What I didn't know then, what I've learned since, is that helplessness has a secretive and deep-seated affinity for freeze. When fighting seems futile and fleeing isn't possible, helpless paralysis takes over. It wasn't that no one else shared these sentiments; it was that they also felt helpless, powerless—frozen.

Helplessness, too, bears a distinct face. Blank, fallen, gloomy, pleading, with hints of fear and glower and mourning. Sometimes it's overcome by words, such as when the command sergeant major lost his composure, pleading with me—"You've got to stop this, sir!"—his distinctly southern drawl strained with incredulity. But more often, the face of helplessness alone fills the bleak funeral home silence, such as when the operations officer—that normally reserved, unflappably impassive man with the polished elocution—and I exchanged uncomfortable glances, the shared emotions of the moment—worry, horror, frustration, desperation, and despondence—emanating from our forlorn eyes, searching from the other an answer to the question, What do we do now? But in the glassy frozen hollowness—that distinctly mournful despondency—neither of us found an answer. Only helpless resignation. Our normal was changing before our eyes.

The apogee finally came one morning when two teammates approached me just after the morning briefing. Written in their eyes was the same weariness, unease, and resignation I found written in the eyes of many that week, the same writing I had seen in the mirror ever since the strike that produced that unforgettable exhale, "That's a kid!" Hovering and speaking in hushed tones, they asked me to review video of an early-morning strike conducted by the subordinate task force in support of its troops on the ground. The figure hidden in the shadows, the waddling toddler, the people obscured under a lush canopy, the falsehoods, the political maneuvering, the unnecessary re-attack, the crowded market, the slender man and lamenting woman and lifeless child—the empty cavalcade of death—it would all lead to this moment.

I stood over the teammate's desk as he pulled up the video, and watched. Five dome-shaped rectangular huts aligned side by side flickered under the familiar spectral green tint of night vision. A mud wall framed the compound, abutting the backside and turning a ninety-degree angle at the rear corner of the farthest left hut. Next to the farthest right hut stood an animal pen, its overhanging brown tarp held up at each corner by what appeared to be rough-hewn poles. A large dirt courtyard stood empty before it all.

Suddenly, like an arrow, came a black projectile standing out in relief against the green-shaded world. Then, a flash as the projectile struck the hut near the ninety-degree angle created by the wall. Then, bits of earth and hut exploded into the air, scattering in dark fragments like a mushroom cloud, before raining down on the earth in a pattern driven by weight and gravity. Then, emerging from the doorway, a phantasmagoric string of humans who, I imagined, had been sleeping peacefully only moments before their world erupted in a flash. Humans who, I imagined, had gone to bed full of food and love and hopes and dreams. Humans who, I imagined, awoke not to a new dawn of dreams and hopes and love and food but to fear and terror and heartbreak.

They emerged slowly at first. A torso reluctantly breaking the threshold: head peering right, then left, scanning for additional danger, unable to comprehend the distorted reality. Then a frantic dash by the uninjured. Even under the spectral tint and midnight sky, I could discern relative age and gender. A few women ran to the farthest hut, their kameezes and burqas billowing gracefully in a graceless night, as the children, whose hands the women held, desperately tried to keep pace; I could hear in my mind the slap of their sandals as they ran, each slap matching the pounding in their chests. A man carrying a child followed the women and children; whether the child was injured, or worse, wasn't clear. Then a second man, supporting a limping third, his right arm wrapped around the waist as his left arm reached across to the limping man's left shoulder.

The strike resulted in civilian casualties. This much was clear, even though the extent was not. And any suspected civilian casualty required reporting to higher powers quickly. This much was also clear.

Yet we hadn't received a report.

I picked up the receiver and called my counterpart at the subordinate task force, trying to calm down as the line trilled, knowing I didn't possess all of the information. Maybe this subordinate commander's team had good reason for striking these people in this hut on this night. I hoped that was the case, that my counterpart could provide context to mitigate the apparent egregiousness.

He answered on the second trill. We exchanged pleasantries. I proceeded to ask him about the strike, my tone unintentionally accusatory. He responded accordingly, sharply. His explanation felt evasive, incomplete, half-baked. I lost my patience, suggesting—no, asserting—the strike caused suspected civilian casualties, asking—no, demanding—he send up the required report.

I tried to be mindful of the team dynamic he faced. He was a good man and attorney, but the previous unit had cut out their attorney, leaving her in the dark and largely ineffective, an unfortunate consequence of providing advice that the team either didn't want or like too many times. My counterpart in this new subordinate unit needed to pick and choose his battles, perhaps a bit more so than I did, or risk suffering the same fate. But there was an electricity to the conversation, the product of growing discontent, and the static carried the agitation in his voice, waiting for the spark that would send an explosion rippling through the cables. I was unsure whether this agitation was directed or misdirected at me, which was only fair, since he was likely unsure whether my anger was directed or misdirected at him.

Before hanging up, he promised they'd forward the required report by the end of the day.

Later that evening, the operations officer and chief of operations asked whether I had received the report. I shook my head and grew uncomfortable, knowing the unspoken expectation was that I call my counterpart to ask the same question. That call would cause more discomfort since responsibility for the report lay with a subordinate operations officer, not that attorney, but I made the call anyway.

He said they were working on the report. Our task force would receive it soon.

His curt "soon" became day two, day three, day four: each day the question asked of me, each day me asking the question of my counterpart, each day the "facts" surrounding the strike changing, shifting, and morphing. The runaround started to feel shady, and soon our higher headquarters began asking about the report, which redoubled the questions from my team, which redoubled my questions to the attorney. "The commander wants to hold off on sending up the report until he can discuss it with the commanding general," my counterpart gruffly apprised.

The report came late on day four.

According to the report, the team on the ground received fire from this compound and requested a strike in self-defense. Ordinarily, though perhaps unjustifiably, such a report would be accepted at face value, generating few questions. After all, no one wants to second-guess the men on the ground facing uncertain death, even when their actions result in unintended and unfortunate civilian casualties. But something about this report didn't sit well. Maybe I had it out for this commander. Maybe my hatred made me want to catch him in a lie. Maybe I wanted him to finally be held accountable for the figure hidden in the shadows, the waddling toddler, the people obscured under a lush canopy, the unnecessary re-attack, the crowded market, the slender man and lamenting woman and lifeless child. But whatever the reason, intuition gnawed. The stomachache returned.

So I dug. I studied the video, watching the thirty minutes leading up to the strike. I received the position of the ground forces and measured the distance between those forces and the compound from which the hostile fire allegedly originated. None of it made sense. The old feeling returned: *Am I going crazy?*

I watched the video three times, five times, ten times maybe, never once observing a muzzle flash or anyone moving in the courtyard. The gnawing stirred doubt. *Is anger contaminating my thinking? Maybe I missed the muzzle flashes or the shadowy enemy firing on our men.* If so, my unfaithful eyes didn't explain how those alleged bullets passed through the eight-foot mud wall separating the opposing forces. *Maybe the enemy fired on our men through firing ports cut into the wall.* But again, I hadn't observed any muzzle flashes from the compound. What's more, even if the enemy had fired toward the subordinate commander's men from within the compound, the firing presented no real threat: at more than one kilometer from the compound, those men were beyond the effective range of the enemy's weapons, meaning this couldn't be self-defense. *They're lying, I'm sure of it. But what if I'm wrong, and they're not?*

The legal issue here concerned more policy than law. A strike can be lawful under the laws of armed conflict yet violate policy directives in a way that ensnares a commander. In many instances, a violator receives some form of mild admonition—a reasonable response in the unreasonable, unforgiving fog of combat—but in the most horrific of situations, particularly those involving egregious conduct, a violator may suffer worse, and rightfully so. While I cannot provide more specifics, here my hairsplitting analysis trained on whether this subordinate task force's strike could be appropriately characterized as self-defense or whether something more was required. The characterization of the strike mattered.

Some might consider this proof that lawyers are the problem, meddling and obstructing the "lawless" arena of combat, handcuffing "us" from defeating "them." That's one opinion, and it's one no lawyer will ever succeed in changing. For the rest, good reasons exist for these policy directives, for circumscribing when and how an individual inhabiting the battlefield lives or dies. Those policy decisions belong not to the lowly lawyer in my position but to the civilian and military leaders at the highest reaches. My role at this level was to faithfully interpret and apply the policies to the facts and to advise.

From without, I analyzed the appropriate procedures for this strike, but from within, something far more unsettling disturbed me. The rub didn't concern policy or law. It concerned truth. And the inescapable conclusion I drew from the report—possibly mistaken, probably not—was this: the subordinate commander and his team were lying, propagating a falsehood to cover tracks that might be exposed in the coming review of the suspected civilian casualties. A one-page report took four days. Four days to create a useful mirage; four days to get the story straight; four days to present a most favorable case in support of self-defense. The crime, if there was one, was in the cover-up.

An irrepressible fire burned in my head, inconsolable anger building to a raging inferno. I only felt rage. Rage over another avoidable catastrophe. Rage over more injuries to innocent civilians. Rage over inaction by the leadership above. Rage over this asshole's utter indifference to human life. Rage over his team's embrace of the same indifference. Rage—pure, unadulterated rage.

I wanted to burn it all to the ground. I had an obligation to report suspected civilian casualties. I had an obligation to ensure truth prevailed even, and perhaps more so, when that truth might cast a long dark shadow over our organization. Sure, facts can be fickle, the truth blurry. But it would be a mistake to view blurred edges as absolute opacity. And here I was being asked to underwrite what I believed to be clear lies; to be a party to their deception; to stand by, ignore, and condone what couldn't possibly be true. It was an imperative I couldn't stomach.

At the same time, I faced the unenviable truth of results. I hoped the senior attorney at my higher headquarters would see through the smoke screen, recognizing a mirage for a mirage. But if he didn't, and I reported my suspicions to the attorney above him or pushed back on the report or called out this subordinate commander as a liar or insisted on deeper investigation or contradicted this senior attorney during his presentation to the civilian casualty review board, I too might suffer the same fate as that previous attorney in that previous unit. I too might become a pariah.

The correct answer was obvious—but how? How could I navigate a minefield of social costs, where each uncertain step seemed fated to explode in a ball of flames and shrapnel, cutting me off at the knees and adding one more entry to the growing ledger of casualties?

A cleverer attorney might have found a way to eliminate the Hobson's choice between truth and personal interests, but fear pulled me close, blocking my view. Unfortunately, fear, that base mammalian response that keeps us safe from harm, can sometimes be a terrible basis for decision-making. Where ensuring truth represented the only correct answer, I haphazardly tried to serve both masters: exposing truth, but without seeming like an angry villager armed with pitchfork and torch. They made me part of their deception, my silence made me complicit, and truth became another casualty.

I met with the senior attorney at our higher headquarters shortly after receiving the report. In those discussions, I offered a different perspective on the report, distinguishing the "possible" from the "couldn't be," but without infelicitously calling out as mendacious the subordinate unit's yarn. Unsurprisingly, this pas de deux along the razor's edge of war and diplomacy failed to move anyone. So when our higher headquarters forwarded the report unchanged save for a few inconsequential revisions, I attended the meeting during which the civilian casualty review board would assess whether civilian casualties resulted from this strike. Since no one seemed to share my concern for veracity, I needed to fulfill that truth-telling function.

But when this senior attorney presented the report without raising the incongruities my investigation exposed, and the board debated truth, fear again counseled silence, a shameful bout of laryngitis brought on by deference to superiors and staying in my "lane." I froze, and the board debated. I remained frozen, and the board adjudicated.

"Inconclusive for civilian casualties," the board members determined before moving on to the next allegation without a moment's hesitation.

Truth died that day, or so I believe. Though the report must have consternated someone at our higher headquarters, because a few days after submitting the report, the subordinate commander invited our operations officer to attend a rules of engagement training session. The subordinate commander billed the training as a monthly event conducted by his attorney, but the suspicious timing and the curious fact that this was the first time we had heard of them conducting ongoing training made it all seem hasty and impromptu. The operations officer invited me and another teammate to join him in attending.

Walking to the subordinate task force's building on that mild August evening, I could sense the uneasiness connecting us. Though the rage I felt after analyzing the report had since reduced to a simmer, it continued to teeter on the edge of a boil, the bubbling broth seething and popping on the surface of my rolling commentary. It wouldn't take long for the simmer to boil over.

Seated around a rectangular conference table with the subordinate commander at the head, we listened to my counterpart narrate a slideshow containing vignettes designed to stimulate conversation and reinforce important rules of engagement. It was all standard fare, except the vignettes were drawn from mistakes that week, not some hypothetical scenarios.

The final vignette featured the strike that formed the basis of the fabricated report. I tried to maintain composure as my counterpart set the scene. The succeeding silent space felt unnatural, tense, defensive—an emptiness of authenticity. None of this subordinate unit's members offered commentary in response to my counterpart's prompts.

The subordinate commander broke the silence, interjecting to reaffirm his men's actions in calling in the strike, while slipping in a tepid reminder to exercise patience on the battlefield. With face flushing, I listened to this dog and pony show replete with smoke and mirrors. *Was this charade his way of apologizing for the recklessness? His way of demonstrating contrition? Or was this the means by which he altered reality, shaped the truth, appeased the general, and demonstrated his "leadership" by feigning appreciation for the laws of armed conflict and the sanctity of human life—or at least the lives of "them"?*

This rancid display—this subordinate commander's obviously transparent attempt at deception—made me want to vomit. But as the three of us talked on the walk back to our building, it seemed that the subordinate commander's slick speech had reassured my operations officer, bestowing not firm conviction necessarily but at least cautious optimism for increased order, discipline, and patience. Again: *Am I going crazy?*

Though the days improved, this had less to do with the subordinate commander than with changing circumstances on the ground. The never-ending week ended as the siege dwindled, fading into the shadows from which it emerged like an unseen youth, a natural conclusion seized as specious validation of his reckless approach. But at what cost? The immediate victory ignored the potential long-term defeat, consequences that would be felt well beyond this subordinate commander's departure, with the families' lives uprooted, forever altered, stoking multigenerational fury.

★★★

Now on the far side of that apogee, I've managed to condense the undulating terrain of emotions that stretch forward from the experiences that week to guilt, shame—and rage. My therapist calls the seeds of those emotions "stuck points"; I call them "my failures." But what I've realized is the rage I felt toward this subordinate commander and his team, about the figure hidden in the shadows, the waddling toddler, the people obscured under a lush canopy, the falsehoods, the political maneuvering, the unnecessary re-attack, the crowded market, the slender man and lamenting woman and lifeless child—it's all somewhat misdirected. The anger, truthfully, is at, is *with* me—anger stirred by the introspective, perpetually vacillating second-guessing: *I could have done more*; then, *I did what I could*; then, *I should have done more* ...

This anger further condenses into dishonor, a thick syrup layered over the guilt and shame, complementing them, intensifying their bitterness. In the face of a dilemma, I knew how I would react. *On my honor*, I promised myself.

Until I didn't. Wading into the frigid ocean of difference between saying and doing, promises made became promises unkept, ifs and thens became meaningless, fight became freeze and silence. In that ocean, honor drowned.

Where does honor go? Does honor sink unceremoniously into the murky depths, burying itself in the sediment, collapsing in on itself as the pressure squeezes and darkness prevails, disappearing entirely, existing no more, incapable of being raised? Or can honor resurface, be revived?

And where did *my* honor go? Did it, too, fall into that hole with the rest of me? Because that lost honor is why I can no longer look into the eyes of my reflection. For if I do, I might see the white fiery truth hidden behind the desperation, weariness, torment, and despair that fills those now-vacant orbs.

When I stare at nothing, searching to fill the vacancy with what was and what will be, I almost cannot recall what I felt in the motionless moments of that week. I can, but I can't. I don't inhabit that body. When the invisible hand flips the projector's switch, the motor revs, the spool whirls and clicks like a card flapping against the spokes of a bicycle wheel, and the flickering dreamscapes begin to play on a violent loop, I watch not through my eyes but from above. From without rather than from within. Removed, distant, disassociated. Out of body. Unable to feel what he feels, unable to observe his thoughts, unable to find his words.

Except I know I hate him, that moron. Because his mistakes kill me.

Maybe I have it out for him. Maybe my hatred makes me want to catch him in a lie. Maybe I want him to finally be held accountable. But whatever the reason, I endure, searching for the answers and honor lost.

The rage is projected outward, yet buried inward. Rage over meaningless deaths. Rage over uncourageous, frozen behavior.

Rage over tepid responses. Rage over inaction and silence. Rage over self-protection and careerism and people pleasing. Rage—pure, unadulterated rage.

But perhaps I should heed the lesson buried deep in my dad's two-sentence message, one he alluded to in a coda, "Forget about it—it's over and time to move on."

No one is perfect, and holding on to the rage is unhealthy. It destroys the soul. I need to accept and move on, to let go and forgive.

"Get used to dealing with morons!" Dad had exclaimed. Apt advice, even when the moron is in me.

7. A Ride on the Tilt-A-Whirl

Thwop-thwop-thwop-thwop-thwop.

The percussive effect of the rotating blades reverberates inside my head as we fly from Bagram to Kabul not long after that longest, heaviest week.

I'm seated uncomfortably on the Black Hawk's sagging nylon seats. The gunner stares out the open door, on guard, providing comfort to the occupants, all of whom trust that behind the mirrored sunglasses, his eyes are rapidly scanning the landscape reflected below for signs of danger, an alertness born of duty and self-preservation, both of which we are now beneficiaries. I turn my gaze from the gunner to that same passing landscape, less alert to signs of danger and more in wonder at what lies beneath.

Our shadow playfully dances and rolls like a floating cloud across the vapid beige and brown and khaki plateaus and farmland below before the terrain sharply, and without warning, juts into the heavens. My body remembers the rise and fall, anticipates every twist and turn, leans instinctively into each as our mechanical leviathan darts through the creases, up and around the imposing snowcapped peaks, peaks that flank our base like a standing Army fortified against the past and future, ready to withstand the newest invaders, sentinels of the watchtower. The fingers and ravines reaching out from those peaks seem reminiscent of terrain I've run before. In another time, another place, I might have bounced joyfully from crag to crag on these mountains. But not here, and certainly not now. There's no joy here.

The thin, cool mountain air whips through the cavernous belly, creating a perceptible change in pressure that feels at once external and internal: pushing in, pushing out, lifting up, pulling down. The whipping air lifts the weight from my body, sucks it through the open sliding door, beckons me.

Emerging from the mountain pass, we enter a bowl surrounded by that same mountain range. What was once farmland and plateaus and peaks and couloirs transitions to a vast city of largely single-story mud and clay and concrete structures. The sun glistens off the rippled surface of a languid, shallow river snaking through the city.

As we begin our descent, the once-blurry details come into focus. Barren soccer pitches. Sporadic tree-lined squares. Roads teeming with laden lorries and dilapidated cars. Billboards advertising mobile phone services and Western cosmetics. Dresses and blouses and trousers strewn across clotheslines, dancing gracefully with intermittent wafts. Mounds of garbage. All of it covered in layers of dirt and dust and filth. The city seems larger on this trip, and I begin to ponder the myriad comings and goings of those below in the intensifying moments before we land.

Fast-forward to several months after that uneventful flight when, during an otherwise-pedestrian early-morning walk half a world away in Georgia, I am unwittingly confronted by this memory. But the images of farmland and plateaus and dirt and peaks and couloirs and pitches and lorries and billboards and clotheslines and garbage and dirt are quickly swept away by the unrelenting undertow of that heaviest week, just before the wave of questions generated by an ocean of toxicity in the brain arrives. *How did I fit into the larger picture? Was I the butterfly naïvely, innocently, yet recklessly flapping its wings? Or was my role in all of this—the war, the death, the destruction—significant only in its insignificance? Was I nothing more than a pock in a long history of pocks dotting this pockmarked landscape? Does that absolve me? Is this my punishment?*

The wave of existential grief bears down, breaks, and pummels me. Out of its frothy residue, the familiar packs of demons resurface. I have become a stranger to myself, my place utterly and hopelessly lost. *What purpose have I now? What place have I left? Is this all that remains? A trudging existence bereft of meaning?*

★★★

My father was a clown.

That's not a figurative statement. Well, it is. Sort of. He loved being the center of attention, making people laugh to the point of tears, drinking, and partying. In short, my father loved acting juvenile well beyond adolescence.

But it's also a literal statement. A Freemason and member of the Shriners organization, he would volunteer each year as a clown for the local Shrine Circus. While my father loved volunteering for charitable causes and bringing joy to young children, my suspicions tell me this annual tradition provided an excuse to unload stress by engaging in some of his favorite pastimes: drinking (not before or during performances, mind you) and grab-assing with friends. Motivations, after all, need not be mutually exclusive.

One of my favorite childhood photos is one in which I'm seated on his lap at the edge of a circus ring under the imposing dome and dangling trapeze apparatuses, he in his clown costume and I in a blue-and-white striped shirt bearing a cartoon bear. Although the photo captures a hidden sadness concealed beneath his heavy makeup and expressive smile, the photo still reminds me of his personality, his spirit, and the many teary-eyed, abdominal-cramping moments we shared in that scant and fleeting period before Alzheimer's obtruded. Moments like the ones that moved between us during our annual visits to an amusement park.

The scene that inescapably played out on these visits featured father and son running amok like untethered children ignoring their parents' sternest admonitions, in an effort to beat the crowds to the tallest, fastest, and wildest roller coasters. We would ride the roller coasters over and over and over again, selecting different cars for different sensations, gasping and laughing as our stomachs became temporarily lodged in our mouths.

After we grew tired of waiting in the growing lines, we'd make our way to the Tilt-A-Whirl. Few, it seemed, appreciated this ride's untapped potential, and the lines, if there were any at all, were always short. As we stood waiting, my father would intensely study the open-faced clamshell cars, seeking out the one that appeared to spin fastest on its axis. Dad would bend forward at the waist until his mouth was level with my ear and, while pointing at the chosen car, whisper, "That one." Naturally, my job was to run to and secure *that* car as soon as the ride attendant unfastened the feeble chain tenuously marking the vague divide between decorous and rollicking behavior. I did so with unchecked enthusiasm and dogged determination.

We sat down in our chosen car and lowered the safety bar. I gripped the bar tightly, with heart racing, impatience growing. When the attendant finally released the brakes, and the circular track began to rotate and rise and fall, the cars would roll slowly in one direction and then the opposite in response to some invisible hand. I watched with growing palpable excitement as my dad developed a feel for the rise and fall, anxiously awaiting his instructions. And then, just as the car crested a rise, he'd yell, "Now!" We'd simultaneously slam our combined weight to one side and reflexively pull on the safety bar for good measure (which, looking back, was utterly pointless), all in an attempt to forcefully impose our will and spin the car in the desired direction as fast as possible to maximize centrifugal force. Over time, I became adept at intuiting our car's will and anticipating his commands, and we would spin and spin and spin and laugh and laugh and laugh from the gravitationally induced giddiness. This gift for reading the car's mind wasn't the result of some scientific prowess on his part. No, it was simply the gift of decades spent acting like a complete child. He was a maven of amusement.

In many ways, being a clown defined my father. Like many in his generation, circumstances as well as surrounding familial, cultural, and societal expectations required that he obtain suitable employment and provide for his burgeoning family. He had married his high school sweetheart, welcomed my brother and quickly thereafter my sister, accepted the mantle of provider, and began slowly climbing the vocational ladder.

Though the man matured, the spirit never did. And no statement better exemplified this childlike spirit than my dad's response to the question of his youngest son, a question spawned by that son's own search for identity, purpose.

"Dad, what did you want to be when you grew up?" I'd ask, often.

"I'll let you know when I grow up."

I, on the other hand, displayed a disposition warranted neither by age nor experience. A deeply feeling, introspective old soul. Too serious and too focused. An eighty-year-old curmudgeon masquerading as a teen, easily annoyed by my peers and their silly, inconsequential, and childish preoccupations. Had I screamed, "Get off my lawn!" the outburst would have shocked few. I engaged in my fair share of juvenile behavior, of course. But in large measure, I felt more comfortable with those outside my cohort. An anachronism betrayed only by a boyish appearance.

Whether my father's adolescent behavior was the wellspring of my aged disposition or whether this disposition flowed naturally from particular idiosyncrasies, ours was a symbiotic relationship. The kid in him reminded the kid in me—on a regular basis—to not be so quick to sacrifice youth at the altar of adulthood, to embrace frivolity, to savor joy and pleasure, to laugh often, to be generously self-deprecating and carefree, to act foolish and graciously afford others the same privilege. The adult in me reminded the adult in him—or so arrogance now reassures—to comport oneself appropriately, to exhibit seriousness and maturity, to embrace introspection, to not mask genuine emotions behind a comedic façade, to model responsibility, to recognize when circumstances required sacrificing humor at the altar of fatherly encouragement, guidance, and wisdom.

But truthfully, my father didn't need me to be the adult. He didn't need reminding. He already understood the delicate balance between acting my age and acting his own, between behaving like a child and behaving like a father.

***

Back home from that early-morning walk, ice clinks into my glass as I stare at a magnetic photo strip hanging on our refrigerator. A memento from a friend's wedding years ago. Before Afghanistan. Before all that.

Photo booths seem to invite immaturity. Sure enough, Marcela and I took one normal photo and three wearing goofy expressions. Those expressions—rolled eyes, mock yelling, tongues protruding—contain hints of my father's clownishness.

I smile, looking at those frozen images, but only briefly. A new thought intrudes on my joy: *What happened to that man? Because I cannot find him anywhere.*

I need help, so I turn to my dad's letters, hoping his words can sift through the fallout left behind by Afghanistan. Those letters contain both humor and sobriety, awakening that idle childhood memory of amusement park trips and reminding me of the dichotomy he lived on a daily basis. That dichotomy bleeds from each page more than twenty years later in his choppy transitions between commenting on the Philadelphia Phillies—"Phillies are still a bunch of Bums."—and facetious updates on my bedroom—"The black looks good. The pink glows with the black light."—to lifelong experiences—"Take it as a learning experience one of many that you will have in your life time."—and holiday absences—"Father's Day wasn't the same without you here, and it was difficult."

Had I only listened more closely, I might have recognized the transcendent wisdom and beauty in my father's balance, his pursuit of joy, his embrace of childlike virtues. And then how might my life have been different?

What he wrote then continues to speak today, as though Dad's alive and not just breathing.

"Second guessing yourself, Drake, everyone does this everyday in their life. That won't change. It's natural to do that …. Remember, you are a good person," he reassures, his voice resounding through the nickname he bestowed in my youth, an eponym linked to my favorite childhood cartoon character and Donald Duck's uncle, Ludwig von Drake.

Am I though, Dad? Because I feel unbraked, spinning out of control on life's Tilt-A-Whirl. My balance imbalanced, my place displaced, my purpose unknown, my fate uncertain.

"Remember me telling you in the car that you will have to dig deep into your inner strength to help you when you get down."

But Dad, what do I do when the raging inferno of inner torment burns away that strength's last remaining fumes?

"All I can tell you is that this feeling is just part of the transition. Unfortunately, we human beings are a creature of habit. We do not like change. Right now, you are going through a big change. There is a lot of uncertainty, fear and strangeness in your life right now."

"I want my life back!" I scream into the void formed by his absence and the part of me that fell away.

Except, maybe that's no longer possible. Maybe I can never have that life back, for that life is unrecognizable, forgotten. Maybe as I wander this world aimlessly in search of my soul, the lingering emptiness is just proof that nothing of the old me remains. Maybe I feel this estrangement because that old soul—the *I*—at long last passed on to the next life, rising as smoke from the ashes, dissipating into the somber silvery sky above. Maybe what I attributed to gravitationally induced giddiness was in reality my soul's earliest attempt at escape.

So maybe this is a rebirth. Maybe a new soul is born. Maybe I need to allow the echo of Dad's voice to coax me from the dark and heavy cavern back into the light. Maybe I need to embrace his childlike spirit.

What is my place in this world? I'm not sure.

"Take one day at a time, you can't do more than that," Dad advises through another letter.

I once was what I am not. I'll never be that me again. That me is forever gone.

And maybe that's okay.

What do I want to be when I grow up? I'm not sure. But I know I want to be healed. Or, to put it a better way, I want to be comfortable with the uncomfortable: the new normal, the new me. To be healed seems like overreach.

Photo courtesy of Rick Gority.

Four generations celebrate the birth of my brother. From L to R: Grandfather, Great Grandfather, Ray, Jr., and Ray, Sr.

Photo courtesy of author.

An early Christmas with Dad. The green slime my mother hated can be seen next to the Ghostbusters' firehouse.

Photo courtesy of author.

Inheriting my father's love of model trains. I can still smell the liquid smoke.

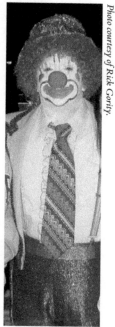

Photo courtesy of Rick Gority.

Reviving the clown costume for my nieces' birthday.

Photo courtesy of Rick Gority.

Epitomizing his "never grow up" attitude.

Constructing the second pond with help from my brother's golden retriever.

Father and son reunited after thirteen weeks at Parris Island.

Author at age seven with Mr. Guinea (seemingly British in my naming conventions; see "Boaty McBoatface"). What's behind those eyes?

Dad and Ray during an annual party. The consumption of alcohol cannot mask the face of pride and love.

Dad in his "cracker jacks" after boot camp.

8. The Pond of Doubt

"How was therapy?" Marcela asks, her voice cutting open the silence, coaxing me from the past out there into the present back here.

She's sitting to my right, leaning forward with forearms resting on her legs, the ghost of a smile flitting across her face. It's a warm weekday evening, and we're on that same covered porch where I broke her heart. In many ways, it's a continuation of that same conversation from September 16th. In many ways, it's always a continuation of that same conversation.

I began cognitive behavioral therapy with the unit psychologist the same month I broke Marcela's heart. Several months in at this point, and the weekly focus on thoughts, behaviors, actions, and how they interrelate didn't seem to be helping. That's what Marcela's asking about now.

"I don't know …" I start, before my eyes dart left, right, up, down, searching the leaves, the weathered fence boards, the trees, and the shadows for the next thought. Marcela checks her voice and waits for me to return, keenly recognizing the need, in this instant, to hold space.

"I don't think it's helping," I continue, plucking the thought from the surroundings. "It's like I can see all the puzzle pieces, see them spread out on the table, but can't figure out how they all fit together. I'm just lost. I don't know who I am anymore."

At its core, moral injury concerns betrayal—by an outsider or oneself. When that betrayal involves deeply held personal values, it can upend identity and efface purpose, with harmful, and too often deadly, consequences.

This crisis over identity and purpose first confronted me while waiting to leave Afghanistan for the last time, then followed me home. It was as though the old me remained behind, forever fated to wander Afghanistan in search of himself, while the new me—the new ship of Theseus—returned to port.

But if purpose hangs on the precipice of identity, then meaning hangs on purpose. And with a splintered identity and uncertain purpose, meaning has now become wanting, and life, as pleasurable as eating with no sense of taste.

Night after night, I go to sleep dreading daybreak. Morning after morning, I wake dreading the day ahead. There's no motivation anymore. Everything has become meaningless, each inane step just another in the inexorable, identity-less march to death's doorstep.

This sense of dread infiltrates every aspect of my life. An endless cycle of dread after dread after dread. I dread running. I dread work. I dread walking the dog. I dread agreeing to meet up with friends, and hard conversations with Marcela, and therapy, and waking throughout the night, and not waking with my alarm, and waking period, and cooking for myself, and unexpected text messages and calls, and responding to emails, and human interaction, and talking, and driving in traffic, and driving period, and work meetings, and running errands, and medical appointments, and visiting family, and hiking, and the future, and the present, and the past. I dread, well, everything.

Except writing. Writing is the one activity I don't dread, the one activity that moves me to action.

I'm not sure why. Perhaps it's because writing restores control and agency, transporting me beyond this 1,260 cm^3 prison cell and providing a temporary reprieve from the ravages of my merciless, obdurate tormentor. Perhaps it's because writing helps slow the thoughts, to unravel and examine each strand individually, to process everything in some neutral way, as though I'm a casual spectator of my own life. Perhaps it's because writing allows me to find myself, wherever I am; to pierce the numbness and feel something— anything—human again. Perhaps it's because writing allows me to find the words and in them, just maybe, some renewed purpose, meaning, redemption. Perhaps it's all of these things and more. It's most certainly because writing is always there, present, ready to witness.

But the words don't come, at least not easily. The proverbial cat with a tongue. It's one of the more frustrating symptoms, one attributable, or so I've learned, to trauma's effect on the part of the brain linked to speech, and even more frustrating in a profession where words and writing are the stock-in-trade. Almost as if the wounds to my soul have induced amnesia, stripping my vocabulary, stealing my voice, and leaving me to wallow inexpressibly alone in the teeming, putrid, infinite wasteland of my mind.

And so it is on that day, in 2019, in Georgia, in springtime, when what I discover staring back is not the reflection of the old me but writer's block.

The cursor's black
heart
pulsating.

Black line

Black line

Black line

Rhythmically blinking,
like a metronome
marking time.
Each flash a laugh,
as the cursor mocks
my fingers
hover
frozen
above the keys.

The words
achingly beyond
reach.

This seems to be the norm now. Like reaching through metal bars, straining, just grazing the skeleton keys that might open the doors leading from this dank, dismal prison. But, unable to force a shoulder through the gap, to gain that extra inch, I surrender as the blinking cursor derides—judges—as if to say, *Come on, spit it out! Do you have nothing to say for yourself?! What a fucking embarrassment.*

That old enemy, self-doubt, returns. The one who followed me through childhood, peddling insults and skepticism, deceits and falsehoods. *You want to win cross-county meets? Impossible. You're too slow. You want to be a marine? Impossible. You're too weak. You want to be a lawyer? Impossible. You're too dumb.*

He's at the threshold now. With each blink, a new criticism. *Who am I kidding?* Blink. *This is foolish.* Blink. *I'm naïve to believe I can make a go at this, write anything that matters.* Blink. *I'm disconnected from reality.* Blink. *I'm engaged in make-believe, a fantasy.* Blink. *Delusions of grandeur.* Blink. *No one will read this.* Blink. *Why bother?* Blink. *You're an imposter.*

These internal waves pound the jagged coastline of my battered heart, leaving behind only a greenish foam of overwhelming despair. And as doubt becomes the only language spoken, I unravel. Truth be told, that blinking cursor—that soulless, pulsating, inanimate object—knows me better than I know myself.

Trying to close the door on this pernicious self-doubt, I open other essays, unpublished and unseen, hoping my words will instill confidence, restore pride, yet finding the opposite: disgust and hatred, adding fuel to the conflagration of self-doubt. *Foolish boy*, self-doubt sneers.

The mocking becomes unbearable. I push back my chair, its wooden legs scraping the woven fibers of my ego, and feel the joints creak as I lift my tired body from the seat. Maybe a walk will clear my head. Then again, maybe not. Maybe it will only feed this corrosive self-doubt a steady diet of salty air. My mind is a form of debtor's prison I can no longer escape—and self-doubt, my vile, abusive jailer.

The self-doubt turns to nihilism as death approaches from the opposite direction. I imagine this undertaking as my coup de grâce, though it will probably never see the light of day. There's just no point. I am laboring toward death. It's only a matter of time.

★★★

I recall asking my father that same question—the one about what he wanted to be when he grew up—many times. It's a conversation I suspect most fathers and sons have at some point during adolescence. More often than not, he would give that same clownish answer. But sometimes, he would let me in, sharing his long-relinquished dream of becoming a journalist. My father never pursued that dream, of course, and whether his non-pursuit resulted from adult responsibilities, self-doubt, or some combination of the two is a truth guarded by the wraiths of the past.

As a child, though, I never once attributed my father's decision to give up on this dream to a lack of ability. To the contrary, I thought highly of his writing, routinely asking him to fulfill the role of copy editor. He'd review my written assignments and research papers, scrawling in familiar handwriting various edits to grammar, spelling, and wording with his trusty mechanical pencil. I'd await his edits with burgeoning anxiety, the value of my writing and self-worth inversely proportional to the amount of graphite wasted on each page.

With the benefit of time and distance, I see that my early impressions of my father's writing abilities were incomplete, based on his short, rhyming motivational notes, scavenger hunt clues, and editorial suggestions, and further skewed by my love and admiration, desire to impress, and need for affection. And, though I find great nostalgic comfort in his letters, time and distance afford this revelation: my father was not a good writer.

That's not to suggest he wasn't talented. It's just his talents lay elsewhere.

We moved four times around central Pennsylvania before my twelfth birthday. I say "we," but I truly mean "my father and I" since our family configuration inhabiting those homes changed through the years: my father, mother, brother, sister and me in the first; father, mother, sister and me in the second; and father, girlfriend-turned-stepmother, and me in the third and fourth. Those homes—the 1970s-style cube home with shake and shingle siding, the stately brick colonial, another hideous 1970s-style cube, and finally a whitewashed ranch—spawn many pleasant memories: my brother killing a snake he found attempting to eat our rabbit; building a treehouse with a Swedish neighbor; an effort to unearth a Native American grave that sent my sister scrambling to halt the excavation; my grandfather setting the grass bank, and later our chimney, on fire; and my father doing cannonballs from our diving board.

Some things trigger these memories easier than others, such as the prefabricated fish ponds and fountains I passed outside a community hardware store once during an erstwhile walk. These ponds and fountains, created with the suburban home garden in mind, never fail as a source of time travel back to my father's creations at two of those four homes.

The first was a small fish pond. He dug the pond by hand, inlayed rubber lining, built a waterfall, installed a circulating pump, filled it with water using a garden hose, and stocked it with goldfish and koi. My father had larger visions, though, and this first pond would pale in comparison to the second.

The second would be far larger, featuring a multitiered waterfall and a small stream looping around to empty into the larger pool. In the center, around which the stream wound, would sit a wooden gazebo accessed by a small arched wooden bridge. This undertaking exceeded the bounds of ordinary hobby and consumed his free time for months.

My father began by renting a mini-excavator to dig a large hole that would eventually form the large pool, the excavated earth pulling additional duty as the foundation for the three-tiered waterfall and gently sloping stream. Once completed, he emplaced large plastic tanks in each waterfall tier; laid the black rubber lining that would contain the water in the waterfall, large pool, and streambed; and installed the pumping system that would feed the falls with a steady flow of water and provide the constant circulation needed throughout the pond for fish to survive.

Around the same time, the gazebo, bridge, and dump-truck loads of large rocks and river stone arrived. With the assistance of my brother and others, we positioned the gazebo on the newly formed island at the center of the design. Then, my father began sifting through the pile of rocks, searching as a child does through jigsaw puzzle pieces for the perfectly sized and shaped rocks to create the waterfalls, form the serpentine stream, and weigh down the edges of black rubber lining the large pool. If a rock didn't exist, he'd swing a sledgehammer, smashing stones until he had chiseled the perfect piece. The image of my father laboring with that sledgehammer under a searing summer sun—his matted salt-and-pepper chest hair, the black cotton shorts stained with paint, white crew socks pulled to mid-calf, the worn and soiled white sneakers, and a paisley bandana folded into a narrow slip and tied just above his brows to keep the glistening sweat from trickling off his bald head and into his eyes—remains branded on my memory.

Once my father found the perfect piece, whether through the hammer or haystack, he'd purposefully position the rock. Then, like a painter carefully contemplating a work in progress, he'd take a few steps back to alter his perspective in search of the bigger picture. The goal, of course, was to make the entire creation appear natural, as if God had created it at the beginning of time.

After satisfactorily arranging the large rocks, my father filled the pool, stream, and waterfall basins with river rock and then, in exchange for a financial donation, had the local fire company fill the pond with water using a tanker truck. All that remained was to emplace the bridge; stock the pond with goldfish, koi, and fantails; and incorporate water lettuce, pickerel rush, water hibiscus, lilies, green taro, and river reed in a manufactured attempt at a natural appearance.

Though my father encountered many challenges, setbacks, and frustrations during the build and again each fall when he renewed his battle against the leaves threatening to clog the water pump, the pond was objectively beautiful, a source of much pride, an oasis of his creation. And the gazebo, around which everything flowed, would eventually become a centerpiece in my young life, serving as the picturesque backdrop for my hopelessly romantic dates, our intimate family breakfasts, and numerous father-son conversations lubricated by coffee and punctuated by the trickle of water. "When you get feeling this way, picture you and me sitting in the gazebo, I'm giving you a motivational talk," Dad reminded me soothingly in one letter.

Walking past that hardware store display, I gained a newfound appreciation for my father's creations. The same time and distance that allowed me to recognize the shortcomings in his writing skills also allowed me to admire his perseverance.

My father designed and built both ponds in the pre-internet age, benefiting neither from home improvement blogs nor do-it-yourself guides available at the stroke of a few keys. He brought these visions to life not through the cheat codes to creation but through raw perseverance: flipping through old issues of home and garden magazines at the library; talking with ecologists; sourcing rocks, stone, tanks, and liners; engaging in a lot of trial and error and learning from mistakes; and, most importantly, never giving up and never giving in on his aquatic landscape dreams.

I suspect my father possessed moments of self-doubt about his ponds and decisions in life in general. It's inevitable. But he also possessed resilience in the face of setbacks and uncertainties: the ability to bounce back when his serpentine stream wouldn't flow because it had too shallow a slope or when the headwaters didn't materialize because water cascaded from the uppermost tank before rising high enough to feed the stream. In those moments, my father summoned the courage to put doubt aside, stomped over to unplug the pumps while muttering a string of expletives, and tried again.

My father persevered because these ponds were his dreams. And in doing so, he created his own oasis—the happiness that existed in his mind and his alone.

★★★

Like his words of encouragement during boot camp, I view my father's model of perseverance through new eyes. Gripping the mane of memories, riding them through writer's block, galloping away from self-doubt and the decisions and failures of Afghanistan.

Still the words don't come. I endure the Sisyphean struggle for a bit before the memories slow to a trot. Self-doubt catches up.

What did Dad tell me during boot camp? I ask.

"Dig deep," he exhorted. "Quit being so critical of yourself. Don't let them get you down. You can do this!"

The gazebo comes into view—Dad's motivational talks. "You're strong don't doubt yourself."

I cannot allow this self-doubt to steal the last remaining oasis of a broken man. Like my father with his backyard ponds, I must push aside the self-doubt. I must find the strength he assured I possess, the strength now buried somewhere deep beneath emotional boulders. I must find the courage I lacked in Afghanistan. I must remind myself of why I'm writing. I must find me again. I must find my identity. I must find my path. I must find healing, forgiveness. I must help others. I must hope, and give hope. I must pull the words, and be pulled. I must.

Because I cannot ignore this pull to something beneath and beyond. I will find the words. I will drag them kicking and screaming and bloodied from the shadowy depths of my wounded soul, allowing them to mend the brokenness. I will expose them to the light and share them so they may comfort other prisoners. I will follow them, wherever they lead, however long it takes. I will

Dad believed in me; maybe I should too. Because if I don't believe in myself, who will believe in me?

Or maybe I'm only fooling myself again.

9. On the Precipice of Life

Seven months after redeploying from Afghanistan, I'm seated in the passenger side of the colonel's silver Prius as we make the four-hour drive west across Georgia. He's focused on the pavement winding and rolling lazily through the rural countryside while I stare blankly out the window at passing loblolly pines and cedars and oaks, the sun's rays filtering through their branches, illuminating the darkness beneath like some manna from heaven.

We've just spent the morning reluctantly revisiting the mountain plateau where the enemy mortally wounded one of our men, and now the thick Georgia air hangs heavy with solemn silence. Like the sun's blinding white rays, my thoughts fill the spaces, weaving through the broken branches of my psyche.

I begin replaying the events of that morning's briefing to the wife of a fallen hero, a morning spent explaining how her husband had died on a different morning, in battle. How she sat wearing an unwavering expression, back straight and stiff, hands resting on the polished wooden table, her body unable to give up any more tears, suspending those remaining above a dark, cold pit in a coffin she did not choose. How she was flanked by tributes to the unit's history, its victories and heroes, and men wearing the same uniform as her dead husband, bearing the same accoutrements and awards and icons, all while this good-natured colonel recounted in painstaking detail how her husband had given his life over, had become one more hero to adorn these walls, one more story in the storied lineage of this unit.

I had been there when it happened. Not *there* there, of course—not on the ground in the firefight but there in Afghanistan. Awoken when he was wounded and when he took his last breath. Present for the cackle on the radio, the urgency of response, the hue and cry for retribution, the pressure campaign, the ensuing rush to death. Standing in formation at his memorial, fixating on the two-dimensional photo that failed to capture his three-dimensional persona as roll was taken and his response noticeably missing. Overseeing the investigation that now served as the foundation for this epilogue, this account of his heroism and last moments, this unfitting elegy expressing unnecessary confirmation of his goodness and sacrifice, his love for family and country.

This briefing would be no epilogue for her, though. Instead, it marked the unwanted prologue to a new book in the story of her life, in the story of her family, minus one. What words, what sentiments could even begin to fill the gaping hole left by his absence, by this grief?

Replaying this scene against the flickering landscape, I am hit by a bastardized version of survivor's guilt. How could this good and honorable family man have his life cut short while others, like me, received an unworthy reprieve that allowed us to carry on, to chase our dreams, to live and to love just a bit more, just a bit longer? It all seems so unfair and tragic.

Only later, after the car ride, did I appreciate the profanity of this thought. I had survived nothing. This thought—this guilt—was nothing more than an unjust, perverse attempt to co-opt her grief. I had that luxury, after all: the luxury of shameful sorrow.

★★★

The summer of 2019 brought a new assignment, a fifth move in seven years that would take Marcela and me roughly six hundred miles north on I-85 from Fort Benning, Georgia.

We drove separately: she took the direct route; I, the more circuitous path through Great Smoky Mountains National Park, hoping the park's sheer proximity might rekindle that once unbridled passion for trail running. Besides, I needed to put some distance between the unit and me, between the past and the future, and getting figuratively lost in the 522,000-plus-acre wilderness seemed like a decent way to escape the no-man's-land of the present.

I had booked a two-night stay in Gatlinburg and began the six-hour drive. Rolling rural hills, the busy ring road encircling Atlanta, and the softly curved peaks of northern Georgia and western North Carolina greeted me before I turned northwest, up and over the mountains straddling North Carolina's border with Tennessee, past Clingmans Dome, and through the throngs of summertime tourists littering the serpentine road's shoulders. The last thirty-some miles between Cherokee, North Carolina, and Gatlinburg, Tennessee, with its dawdling drivers, halfhearted hikers, and clueless crowds scurrying about like frenetic squirrels in the face of oncoming cars, brought about sighs, grumbles, hand gestures, slaps of the steering wheel, and the nightmarish premonition that silence would be crowded out by obnoxious racket.

Arriving in Gatlinburg did little to assuage any foreboding. Garish faux log cabins, flashing lights, and kitschy storefronts attempted to lure me into this fabricated world, and my heart sank with the disappointing realization that the vision for these two days would not match reality. I should have known better.

After checking in at the hotel and dropping my bags in the room, I returned to the lobby to wait for a trolley downtown. I didn't want to sequester alone, in the room, with my thoughts, treating this as little more than a waypoint on my journey to a new assignment in Virginia, where Marcela and I would live separately for the first time in eleven years. I needed coffee and a space to write.

While waiting for the trolley, I began flipping through the glossy pages of a local tourist magazine. Sandwiched somewhere between advertisements for Ripley's Believe It or Not! and Ober Gatlinburg was an article proclaiming the five "best hikes" in the Great Smoky

Mountains. Knowing from experience that "best" also tended toward "heavily trafficked," but with limited time and a dizzying array of options, I snapped a photo of the list. A useful jumping-off point.

When the trolley arrived, I hopped aboard with a dozen other cackling, sweaty tourists, selecting a seat as far as possible from the others and gazing out the window, hoping to signal an unwillingness to entertain conversation, counting the seconds until I could step off the bus. I had chosen the Great Smoky Mountains for silence but had yet to escape the noise.

The local Starbucks only further proved the rule. Surrounded by giggling and gossiping teenagers, desultory women wearing straw cowboy hats with curled brims chosen for the style but not the life, and chauvinist men in tank tops festooned with neoprene sunglass straps resting on the leathery skin of their necks, I tried to filter the noise through headphones, to tap into my thoughts, to write. But hard as I tried, I couldn't.

I slipped the laptop back into my black canvas backpack, picked up my phone, and started looking through the trails mentioned in the magazine. Below the boldface name of each trail was a paragraph blurb that described its length, elevation change, and the characteristic that made this trail deserving of its inclusion as one of the "best." To buttress the author's unchallenged assertion, editors had carefully curated an inline image highlighting the identified characteristic. It worked, of course, and I found myself drawn to Charlies Bunion.

Charlies Bunion is an out-and-back trail that begins at Newfound Gap. For four-plus miles, the trail hugs various ridgelines as it rises and dips like a roller coaster's first hill, taking hikers above six thousand feet before depositing them on a rocky outcropping with breathtaking 270-degree views of the surrounding mountains and valleys.

Because of the views offered by Charlies Bunion and the crowds encountered on the drive that morning, I anticipated a trail packed with hikers. While other less-trafficked trails could be found, the previous year's wildfires had thinned nearby options, a double whammy since the closures funneled the same high demand into a much smaller supply.

Still, Charlies Bunion met my basic criteria: I could reach the trailhead with minimal driving time, allowing a later wake up and cutting down on the potential post-run road rage that would quickly eliminate any endorphin boost; the trail was of ideal length and elevation gain, providing some challenge while limiting risks in light of the limited running gear on hand; and the effort would be rewarded with an incredible view across the Smoky Mountains, a decadent dessert for a hungry soul. And so Charlies Bunion it would be.

I woke early the following morning. With dawn breaking over Gatlinburg, I stood on my hotel balcony with a fresh cup of coffee, looking out across the sleepy town to the quietly watching mountains, their smoky gray comforter pulled back just so, allowing the warm salmon glow to filter through, arcing across the curtains of sleeping eyes and slowly coaxing them from their dreams. I've always enjoyed this early-morning silence, the stillness that nestles while the rest of the world rests. Life just seems to move slower.

On this morning, I felt content to enjoy the tranquility, to catch my breath after running nonstop for years. But I needed to get on the road if I was to preserve any scattered hope of finding this same stillness waiting on the trail. After refilling the beige polystyrene foam coffee cup, I jumped in the car and began driving to the trailhead.

There were only a few cars when I arrived at the obtusely shaped parking lot a half hour later, buoying hope that the previous day's premonitions would be incorrect, that fate could still be altered. The gentle mountains peaked above the surface of a sea of fog filling the valley below, and I spent a few moments in awe before locking the car. The high tenor beep-beep broke the surrounding silence, like a starter pistol, and I was off.

With each footfall and labored breath, the tension released, slowly, as though the trees and rocks and twigs and roots were absorbing every bead of stress, anxiety, and despair. I didn't encounter another person the entire run. Just me and my shadow. And as time and distance faded, becoming abstract and meaningless concepts, I lost myself in the desolation.

It wasn't long before I reached the final approach to the bunion. Signs admonished visitors to closely control children, alluding to the danger presented by the rocky outcrop and steep drop-off. Heeding the warning, I slowed to a walk to skirt the crags and imposing boulders on this last narrow stretch.

The spur led to the base of the bunion. As the summer heat and humidity pressed down, displacing the cooler air trapped on the valley floor, the fog dissipated, leaving behind only the Smokies' telltale plumes floating among and above the treetops, like melancholy clouds of exhaled cigarette smoke hovering above a bar's patrons.

Scaling the namesake jagged rock, I stood on the precipice, overcome by my insignificance, little more than a fledgling seed sprouting from the earth. Stretching out before me in every direction was a yawning expanse of virgin forest. The neighboring ridges jutted out like rheumatic fingers reaching, straining to touch the horizon. The patches of billowing, ghostly smoke flowed gracefully through the trees and up and over the soft ridgetops, aerodynamically tracing their outlines, exposing the wind's breath.

The smoke's flow reminded me of a dream I once had. In that dream, I stood on a similar precipice, watching as a torrent of emotions jumbled together in a mass of words—words like *disgust, sorrow, misery, guilt, shame*—poured over the edge like a cascading waterfall into an unseen abyss. The dream woke me, and as I lay in bed in a state somewhere between sleep and consciousness, I felt the weight of these emotions pulling me down, powerless to stop the cascade.

Back on Charlies Bunion, I looked over the edge at the trees below, the distance creating the illusion of diminutive saplings, as though I were peering down on the trees of my father's sprawling basement model train display. Suddenly, I felt the conifers' spindly outstretched arms reaching for me—beckoning me to join them, to give myself over, to return to nature.

The French call it *l'appel du vide*. I tried to distract myself from the urge to jump, to throw myself from this rock into the waiting arms below. I turned back to the smoky vapors, imagining them carrying away the last remnants of stress and anxiety and despair. But they seemed to mimic instead the smokiness clouding my mind, casting a dark, pale shadow over me. The pull of the trees, of gravity, returned. "The call of the void."

How easy it would be, I thought, visualizing it all. The weightlessness as my body fell through the air, the liberation, the view as the ground rose up to meet me, darkness replacing darkness. *Would my body be impaled on one of the spires? Would the outstretched arms arrest my fall? Would I bounce from limb to limb like a human Plinko chip on* The Price Is Right? *Would death come quickly, or would I be crippled, writhing on the forest floor, left to die a slow, excruciating death?*

It all started to feel too real, too inescapable. I began to worry that if I thought about it any longer, I might be unable to step back from the edge, might "slip" and begin the descent before I had mentally prepared for the end. I needed to get away from this edge quickly. I took one last look at the horizon before running away from the menacing thoughts.

The parking lot was full of visitors when I returned, a reality that smacked me in the face without warning, as though the trailhead provided some hidden soundproof barrier between silence and chatter, peace and turmoil, fantasy and reality. And as I returned from the brink and crossed this mystical barrier, I reentered the real world. A world brimming with screaming children weaving wildly between clusters of conversing adults, young couples loaded down by overflowing packs, mothers and fathers sporting baby carriers and gripping the upper arms of aging parents. A world of walking sticks and cameras and sunscreen and hats and sunglasses and laughing and smiling and joy. A world of families. And me, alone.

★★★

My father loved *National Lampoon's Christmas Vacation*. Every holiday season, we'd sit and watch Clark Griswold's futile attempts to give his family "the hap-hap-happiest Christmas since Bing Crosby tap-danced with Danny-fucking-Kaye."

Certain movies lend themselves to repeat viewings. *A Christmas Story, Willy Wonka & the Chocolate Factory*, and *Super Troopers* are a few personal favorites. *National Lampoon's Christmas Vacation* is no different. Even when we can quote the movie's parts verbatim, these timeless movies somehow still make us laugh.

I remember watching *National Lampoon's Christmas Vacation* with my father. He'd carefully arrange a few logs in the fireplace and patiently set to work starting the fire. Once the flames began flickering and dancing to the music of wood crackling, we'd find a comfortable spot and settle in for our unofficial annual viewing. As familial love warmed our hearts and the fire's radiant heat our bodies, I'd gleefully anticipate the funniest moments, turning to watch as his head tilted back, his belly bounced, and he wiped tears from the crinkles formed at the corner of his eyes. Over time, my joy became less about the lines themselves and more about my father's infectious response: the guttural laugh, the twinkle in his eye, the living embodiment of Thomas Nast's portrayal of *Merry Old Santa Claus.* That laugh and that twinkle became the visual personification of the Christmas spirit.

While I am certainly neither the first nor the last to declare that my father epitomized Clark Griswold, in my mind the two were synonymous in spirit. My father represented "the last true family man." He cherished family; that "one big, happy family" in many ways representing his lifelong dream.

My stepmother and I met my father one evening at Olive Garden, the ubiquitous chain that passed for fine dining in our small community. Having just attended a funeral for an Italian-American friend, my father arrived wearing a double-breasted charcoal pinstriped suit. The suit was a change from his normal nonbusiness attire: the brand-name polo shirt tucked into khaki shorts and secured with a black braided belt, the entire ensemble further accented by a pinky ring, Masonic ring, wedding band, and gold bracelet.

As we passed the endless breadsticks and soppy salad, the scent of his musky cologne permeating the displaced air, my father passionately described the funeral scene: the beautiful Roman Catholic cathedral, the pews packed with family and friends, the elegiac tone. But one thing in particular stuck with him. As he made his way through the receiving line to pay his respects—a line that stretched from nave to apse—the deceased's family members shook his hand, expressing not their gratitude for my father's attendance but sorrow for his loss. They kept saying, "I'm sorry," to my father as though it were his relative who had passed. It left an indelible impression on him.

"*That's* 'family,'" he declared, before washing down a bite of garlic bread with a mouthful of his favorite rosé.

The makeup of our family changed over the years. My parents had divorced when I was eight. Though the details surrounding their crumbling marriage came nearly three decades later, I can recall the signs that portended the pending collapse.

Shortly after their divorce, my father began dating a woman whom he'd later marry. A widow, her previous marriage had resulted in three children. Seemingly overnight, my family doubled in size, a change both exciting and overwhelming.

Her children were slightly older than my brother and sister. And while my brother, sister, and new siblings enjoyed their young adult lives, I enjoyed my life as an "only child." Over time, marriages gave birth to a familial supernova as one brother and sister became five brothers, five sisters, four nieces, and a nephew.

My father couldn't have been happier. He was a grandfather and could lay claim to the blessings afforded by his rightful status as "pappy." His children gifted him with five—and eventually eleven—grandchildren to love and adore and spoil and dote on. My father was, to borrow the expression, in hog heaven.

The use of "his children" above is no accident. There can be a tendency, a natural unacknowledged yet uncharitable inclination in family mergers, for an adult to view their biological children and grandchildren as "perfect" and their stepchildren and step-grandchildren as "imperfect." But, true to his character, that wasn't my father. Though only three children shared his blood, all six received his unconditional love. He never once treated my stepmother's children as *hers*. He never treated her biological children disparately. He never treated certain grandchildren more favorably than others. All of the children and grandchildren, whether of blood or marriage, were *his* children—*his* family—and equally so.

No holiday epitomized family more for my father than Christmas. All year he'd save his vacation days until December, when he'd take off most of the month to spend each day at home with family.

Like Clark Griswold, he spent the first few days of that vacation focused on the symbolic. First, the decorations. After his morning coffee, he'd venture outside into the crisp winter air, climb a ladder, and arrange strings upon strings of white twinkling lights on the roof. Although he remained a traditionalist at heart, his display became more elaborate over time, adding icicle lights (but always white), lawn decorations (but never tacky ones), and, if he were feeling particularly frisky that year, subtle motion lights. While his light display never resulted in a fall from the roof (miraculous, to be honest), never caused the need for auxiliary nuclear supply (to our knowledge), and never blinded neighbors (there's no evidence, at least), his extravagant display, which could be seen from nearby roads, managed to attract attention. He'd stand in the kitchen peering out the bay window, hands cupped around a mug of coffee, warm pride spreading into a slight smile seen through the drifting steam, as car after car drove slowly down our dead-end gravel alleyway to catch a closer glimpse.

My father's focus then turned to finding the perfect Christmas tree around which our entire family would gather as December grew long and the days short. Finding the perfect tree took on a Goldilocks-level analysis. *The tree can't be too small, but it can't be too large or else there won't be room for the presents or to sit. What type? Maybe a balsam or Douglas fir instead of a Fraser fir. The dark green color is better, and the Fraser's needles dropped too quickly last year. What about a blue spruce? The bluish tint might feel like snow, and who knows whether we'll have snow on Christmas. Is this tree full enough? Is this one oddly shaped?*

This was only the beginning of my father's endless, exhausting examination. Once we found the "perfect" tree—and let's be honest here, he never found the "perfect" tree—his focus shifted to placing it in the "perfect" position. *Turn the tree this way. No, there's a gap in the branches. Turn it to the right. No, a little left. A little more. This branch hangs a bit low; let's hide that in the back. Did you turn the screws on the base? Hold the tree while I tie this fishing line to the curtain rod to keep it standing upright*. I won't even begin to describe the decorating process, which naturally left its mark, much to Marcela's frustration every year when we decorate our Christmas tree.

It may seem like I'm complaining. Hell, in the moment, I probably *did* complain, sighing and rolling my eyes with each new criticism or unsatisfactory change. I just wanted to play video games, and this was all taking too long!

Time warps perspective though. And now I cherish those moments with a nostalgia born of a simpler time. Because for all the individual and shared frustration, impatience, and annoyance, there existed equal parts joy, laughter, and delight. We were a family. We were together. We were home.

Home. How do we define this word? Merriam-Webster defines the noun as "one's place of residence," "the social unit formed by a family living together," and "a place of origin"; the adverb as including "a vital sensitive core"; and the adjective as "of, relating to, or being a place of residence, place of origin, or base of operations."

Yet none of these definitions adequately capture this amorphous, sometimes ephemeral, always ineffable experience. That hasn't stopped countless others from trying. Whether Pliny the Elder's "home is where the heart is" or Emily Dickison's "where thou art, that is home," most people can parrot a favored stock phrase, an overused cliché. The trouble is that clichés lose their emotive power with each overuse on mass-produced faux farmhouse decor. What was once profound soon takes on a shallowness devoid of fervor.

Defining "home" in the negative seems easier. It's not just physical; it's not just four walls and a roof; it's not just a birthplace or a city; it's not even necessarily where one resides. It's mental, emotional: a state of being and a state of living. So how can one define this state in a way that truly encapsulates and conveys the breadth, and depth, and warmth, and comfort, and all the other untold emotions felt when one has found home? Words and their employers are simply too feeble, too inadequate to describe this complex human experience and emotion. Maybe that's why we resort to clichés.

Home is something you know only when you feel it. It's the soothing warmth that spreads slowly through the gullet with that first spoonful of soup after a day in the biting winter cold. It's the contentment, safety, and security felt while entwined with a lover under clean cotton sheets as the early-morning light peeks through the blinds and casts an easy glow across the bare floor. It's the transcendent peace experienced from a rock ledge overlooking an alpine lake framed by mountain peaks as the wind soughs through eavesdropping evergreens. It's the simple bliss felt when, on a brisk morning, the rising sun's rays first kiss your skin as you emerge from a darkened tent. It's a fluidity shaped and defined by our unique experiences, a concept that means one thing today but something entirely different in five, ten, fifteen years, shifting unnoticed like the sand under a swelling sea.

Back in that childhood home, and once finished with the tree and exterior illumination, my father turned his attention to shopping. Shopping for gifts, just as with his tree selection, took a varied approach. Sometimes he'd order gifts from department store catalogues. Sometimes he'd drive to the shopping mall in the neighboring city. And once internet shopping became ubiquitous, he'd browse eBay in his tighty-whities and frayed white cotton V-neck T-shirt.

But every year, we'd take a few shopping trips together. I'd arrive home from school as the sun dipped below the horizon, its warmth and light obscured by a blanket of gray clouds, and we'd hop in the car for the twenty-minute drive to the shopping mall. As nightfall came, I'd watch out the fogged window as barren trees and the once-pure snow now defiled by plows and gravel and salt flashed by under highway lights, stifling laughter as my father beat on the steering wheel drum set and sang along with Frankie Valli, his neck tightening and tendons popping, head tilting and face contorting as he tried to match the crooner's trademark falsetto.

Invariably, my father's mission on those trips involved jewelry. He'd park the car, and we'd find our way into the warm haven afforded by the big-box building. I was embarrassed to be out with my dad.

I wanted nothing more than to strike out on my own in search of pretty girls—to whom I would not speak, of course—but, much to my teenage chagrin, there would be no deviation from the path to his objective.

Occasionally we'd scour the jewelry displays in search of the perfect gift, but most of the time my father already knew what he wanted to buy. He would identify a few rings or necklaces or earrings or bracelets and ask the young, typically attractive, female sales clerk to remove them from the display for closer viewing. He'd examine them closely, as though he were the world's foremost expert on gems and settings, and I'd feign interest; my attention, guided by teenage hormones, was directed to the cute girl browsing a neighboring clothing rack.

What I remember most, though, is what would happen next. With the options displayed atop the glass counter, Dad would look over and, using that familiar nickname, ask, "What do you think, Drake?"

My father knew I didn't know the first damn thing about jewelry. My opinion was as uninformed as Ptolemy's opinion of the solar system. Yet he—my father, not Ptolemy—included me in the decision-making process anyway. And, in doing so, he packed my opinions with consequence. To a teenage boy secretly desperate for his father's love and affection, the opportunity to influence my father's decision made me feel special and respected.

Of course, I frequently, though unintentionally, recommended the more expensive item. A facetious, exasperated moan would escape his mouth. He'd turn back to the display, stare at the items for a minute or so in focused contemplation and finely attuned inspection, and push his choice toward the sales clerk. More often than not, he chose the piece of jewelry I had recommended.

Once the sales clerk had wrapped the item, we'd go to dinner at TGI Fridays or Applebee's or some other pervasive chain. Sometimes I wonder whether he regretted asking for my opinion given my proclivity for choosing the more expensive items, but part of me also suspects he relished the paradoxical opportunity to impress the young sales clerk with his expensive purchase.

These shopping excursions personified his cognitive dissonance surrounding displays of love. While he regularly espoused that money can't buy love, he seemed to spend a lot of money on material things in an attempt to achieve just that. Jewelry was his go-to gift to this end.

It wasn't conscious, though. He truly did believe that money can't buy love. It's just that sometimes he lived in the disconnect, struggling with the nonmaterial displays of love and emotions. Material gifts became an easy means for outwardly manifesting his inner world.

We all fall into this trap. At some point in our lives, we all use material gifts to emote love. That's not to suggest that material gifts aren't valuable or cherished in their own right; they can be. But, as hackneyed as it may be, true intimacy and love, whether romantic or familial, lives in the act and not the gift. It's the verb, not the noun. And, for all his cognitive dissonance, for all the moments he lived in this disconnect, if we set aside our grievances and personal pain, if we remain fair and just and unemotional in our appraisals of the man, none of us could ever question my father's love. Because my father never forgot the true spirit of Christmas. He never forgot that the light of Christmas Day shone brightest through the nonmaterial and sentimental displays.

For the most part, my father gave his family both in abundance. He did so intentionally, such as through the short handwritten motivational notes he'd leave for me the morning of a cross-country meet or the scavenger hunts he'd contrive for my stepmother, leading to some hidden present. But he also did so unintentionally, through shared moments, such as the time he spent at home during the Christmas season and our joint shopping excursions. These shared moments—just he and I—represent some of the greatest, most treasured gifts he ever gave me. Because in these moments, he gave me that most valuable of commodities, that greatest gift any human can ever give: his time.

This gift my father understood. He intuitively understood the value of shared moments. Although he loved receiving a new train for his collection or a piece of circus memorabilia, what my father loved more than anything was time spent with his family. And for this reason, he cherished Christmas Day above all others.

I remember waking on Christmas morning as a nine- or ten-year-old and rushing out to the living room to discover the mountain of presents. The stacks stood taller than my diminutive frame and deeper than the average adult, as though Santa had spent the entire night at my house, carefully arranging the presents into separate groups for each child and grandchild. Of course, I knew it was my father and not some mystical bearded man in a red suit. And, as the years passed, I took on the role of elf to my father's alter ego, helping to assemble and group the packages for the following day's gathering.

Those gatherings were chaotic. Family members would arrive in the early afternoon. We'd spend time gathered around the kitchen island, the endless conversations shattering the easy morning silence. I tried, as any young boy might, to find my place in these conversations. Too young for the adults but too old for the grandchildren, I often just listened and observed as my father laughed and my stepmother attended to the turkey, its aroma wafting through the house.

A particular warmth would spread throughout the house on this afternoon more than any other. It was more than the warmth of bodies packed together in a relatively enclosed space, or the oven cooking for hours, or the fire in the hearth. No, this was something larger than all those combined. It was a magical, spiritual, radiant warmth. A warmth incapable of superficial creation. A pureness that emanated from simple love, joy, and happiness.

In one of his letters, my dad wrote: "You, ray, grandkids are my life. Remember the Marines have you now but I have you always."

His *life*. In the rearview mirror of wistful escapism, my father's wording finally makes sense, a semantic choice exhibited best in the pageantry that followed when the family—*his* family—moved into the living room on Christmas Day.

There, my father would take his place on the reclining chair, gripping a refreshed cup of hot coffee perched precariously on his leg and, with the air of a patriarch, waving his hand to direct the distribution of presents. We'd ravenously tear into the presents, transforming the living room into a mass of boxes and toys and dolls and clothing and shredded paper that obscured the golden oak floor, and he'd watch with a smile so spontaneous and true that even the best actor would be hard-pressed to re-create it. A smile that revealed the great pride and deep satisfaction he experienced in giving to those he loved more than he could ever love himself. His grandchildren would run over and hug their "pappy." His children would express gratitude. And in this moment, though he never expressed it as such, I believe my father received the only gift he ever truly desired: to be surrounded by his family. For in these moments with family, my father's tired soul received the nourishment it desperately needed. My father may not have been wealthy, but in these moments, he was rich in life. No material gift could ever compare.

Regrettably, this tradition faded as his children and grandchildren grew and built their own lives, routines, families, and traditions. Year by year, Christmas afternoon became less and less chaotic, less a gathering and more a smattering of random comings and goings. I cannot help imagining my father longing for the days when his entire family gathered for one unforgettable afternoon, concluding that, with each passing year, my father's heart grew heavier, his soul wearier as the only gift he desired remained ungiven.

For my own selfish peace of mind, I can only hope the memories of those Christmas gatherings buoyed his waning spirit. Because, although I may be incapable of adequately defining "home," I know that Christmas with my father—the tree, lights, decorations, fire, gifts, movies, food, laughter, love, and time—was where my heart lived and soul glowed. We were his life; we were his home.

***

I am no longer staring out that car driving across Georgia, no longer standing on that precipice above a sea of evergreens, no longer sharing Christmas traditions with my dad. Those things occupy the past. Yet something from those experiences remains. Rooted firmly in the present. Like some smoky apparition, haunting me.

Shame, that insidious bastard—that's what remains. Shame that the hero, who was more deserving to live, died; and that I, who am less deserving to live, did not. Shame that I had co-opted his wife's grief. Shame that I did not make the most of my time with my father, that good and honorable family man. Shame that I did not relieve the burdens on myself and others by stepping off that precipice.

But shame cuts both ways. The shame that pulled me to leap is the same that held me back. Depriving one more family of a member, adding one more loss to the war's merciless tally, causing more pain to those who love me didn't seem to be the way to honor that Ranger's sacrifice, his family's grief, my father's life.

I think about the wife of that fallen hero often, if not every day. Though our circumstances differ, I can empathize with her. The emotions and pain surrounding loss represent a great universal truth. And while I don't know this with any certainty, I suspect what sustains her in the aftermath of her husband's death is what gave my father life, is what saved me that day on Charlies Bunion: family.

Family can tear us apart and mend; can be the organism for which we die and live; can be elegy and epilogue. And as Dad stressed to me in one of his letters, "That's why family is so important."

10. The Nuance of Worth

Eight months after moving from Georgia to Virginia, the first snow arrives. I drive to a nearby trail. To walk, to think. Family may have delivered me from Charlies Bunion, but that also meant the guilt and shame of Afghanistan survived.

The snow plumes effetely, unceasingly, like a thousand sacks being emptied, and alights on the outstretched arms of naked oaks, embellishing their cracked skin with pillowy purity and blanketing the forest in a white duvet of silence. The untrammeled quilt stretches before me in every direction, punctuated only by the crumpled leaves and hollow trunks and arthritic twigs—the patchwork detritus of seasons past—and the sonorous creak underfoot as my weight settles on the weathered floorboards of this wild home.

The submissive quarter-sized flakes stick to my jacket sleeves before the edges of each crystalline structure shrivel, dying a slow, painless death, as though I am watching a time-lapse video. I hold out my hand in a futile attempt to forever capture this fleeting tranquility, innocence.

Turning clear against my black gloves, the crystals appear as if they're made of spun sugar, the dendrites reaching outward from the nucleus, piercing the honeycomb lattice like miniature frozen arrows through the heart. Each represents a single droplet surrendered to the pull of the frigid air, growing concentrically as ripples from a rock tossed into a lake. And I am struck by how each flake unabashedly parades its unique imperfections before collapsing in on itself, only to be swiftly forgotten and replaced by another, and another, and another, each but a mere flash in the pan of an impermanent life.

Oh, to be so soft, so pure, so immaculately flawed.

★★★

For all his strengths, my father's feet were still made of clay. A study in contrasts between the kind, jovial, good-natured man I loved and the angry, baleful, bitter man I feared.

For one, my father could erupt in startling anger, an uncontrollable tendency that became all the more pronounced in the middle stages of his Alzheimer's; an anger displayed perfectly in one unforgettable, unpleasant childhood memory indelibly imprinted on the pages of my book and repeated many times thereafter; an anger that adds texture and depth to the portrait of a flawed man.

My bedroom in our second home—the one that was to represent the achievement of his middle-class American dream and supply his elusive happiness—sat at the top, and slightly to the left, of an oak staircase. Upon entering, a visitor would find my twin-size bed and cartoon comforter positioned flush with the wall in the left-hand corner, toy trains, firetrucks, ambulances, and action figures strewn about the room. I had probably already lost the privilege of playing with the Ghostbusters-branded slime that went with my Ghostbusters firehouse, an unfortunate by-product of my mom's growing ire at finding the green goo matted in the carpet's fibers. And though many happy memories hang in that bedroom like the ghosts of history, forever inhabiting the walls of an ancient building, connecting the past and present for generations, they cannot ward off the shadows that lurk after lights-out.

I must have been five or six years old the night when, through the shared wall separating my bedroom and their bathroom, I heard the screaming, the yelling, the crying, the pounding, the shattering, the violence, the pain, the terror, and the betrayal. I had lain in bed, little heart racing, slender body shaking, rotund face swollen and wet. Unable to sleep, unable to understand, unable to intercede.

I don't know what precipitated that fight, one of many between Mom and Dad over the years, but I know the wall offered that little boy no protection from the dark shadows. And I can't help but think the screaming, the yelling, the crying, the pounding, the violence, the pain, and the terror remains trapped somewhere among the studs and space hidden behind the drywall—a permanent fixture in the history of that home, and me.

My father's abusive temper affected not only his first marriage, inexorably contributing to its demise, but also his relationship with his children. My brother, who possesses more than a decade of experience over me, occasionally relates how the discipline I received under my father's hand during childhood paled in comparison to the discipline he received; how my father had become "soft" with age, how my brother had it "much worse," as though this were some sort of sadistic competition involving the severity of corporal punishment. I am, of course, unable to contradict my brother's recollection with empirical evidence, and he offers none, but that doesn't mean I didn't suffer my father's anger, however mollified it may have been.

Most of the time, my father's anger was loud, sudden, what you might expect from an explosion. But it could also be silent, a noticeable change in temperature read in nonstandard behavior, presaging some undesirable consequence to come and one my father expected would speak for itself. Over time, I developed an intuition for my father's emotional state and whether the sound of my or any other voice might precipitate unwarranted anger, a prescience that came to define the contours of our relationship. It's the intuition developed from accrued experience, that painfully efficient pedagogue who teaches through lectures and gestures, stinging skin and salty tears, fear and rejection.

During boot camp, Dad wrote, "When I leave work, I forget about it. That's what you will do when you finish boot camp." But did he? Because my childhood pedagogue taught otherwise. I learned to read the cues as my father walked from his car into the house after a day at work, the tenor of his day and resulting approachability measured in the furrow of his brow, the purse of his lips, the heat radiating from his dark chocolate eyes; in how a lack of any greeting objectified a giant Do Not Disturb sign, his unspoken need for silence unmarred by a stream of questions or endless rambling; in how a brusque response to the dogs barking as he entered the house betrayed a volatility best avoided by remaining sequestered in my room; in how his speaking to me in barely stifled tones through clenched teeth like a cornered animal signaled the need to withdraw until the threat passed; in how a request to take a ride with him, when coupled with no music, no speaking, just a supernatural calmness, sounded like a bad omen.

If I'm honest and objective in this account, my father's anger and frustrations in life, the ones that boiled over and found a misplaced outlet in his family, that sacrosanct unit for which he possessed and professed a deep-seated love, pushed me away from that love and into fear's arms. I learned to approach my father cautiously, anxiously, hesitatingly so as to avoid his wrath and a wounded heart. And, gradually, this cause and effect forged a yawning chasm between father and son, between him and me—one that swallowed our yearning for closeness; one that now can never be closed.

His anger and the consequent tiptoeing tarried below the surface of my childhood, hidden in the ways it influenced personality and behavior, the paradigmatic nurture to one's nature, whereas other memories stand above. Like when my father found flow in his stained-glass hobby, a transcendence of sorts, freeing him from the darkness and his shortcomings.

I would sit by my father's side for what felt like hours, watching as he deliberately, meticulously worked to breathe life into his stained-glass design. Though the memory of his designs faded long ago, lost to life's slowly setting sun, the sights and sounds and sensations loom dormant, waiting for the reminder that vibrantly arouses, bringing them into the forefront of consciousness from deep within the recesses of my brain: the wire mesh side shields of his gunmetal-colored safety glasses, evoked by a screen covering an open window on a breezy summer evening; the feel of art glass under my fingers, raised by the undulating surface of a frozen lake; the microfractures under the glass cutter's carbide wheel, echoed in the cracking of that lake's frozen surface; the strike of the steel ball along a scored line, replicated in a bird tapping on a windowpane; the splitting of a glass piece into two, reproduced in the snap of a twig underfoot; the vibrations and high-pitched whir of a glass piece being smoothed against a spinning stone wheel, reverberated in the dentist's drill; the drawn and redrawn design stencils, mimicked in the faint, un-erased traces of carbon lingering in the rough pulpy creases of sketch paper; and the touch of spooled solder wire to the iron's heated metal tip, imitated in the sizzle of cold bacon on a hot griddle.

On the rare occasion when he had patience in abundance, my father would describe each step, explain his techniques, and answer my inane questions. Sometimes he'd allow me to score a discarded piece of glass, smooth edges using the stone grinder, or solder a joint. But even when he didn't, I enjoyed the simple pleasure of spending time in my father's presence, watching him practice his craft while rolling the residual silver solder beads between my thumb and forefinger.

My father, like most artists today, used machine-manufactured art glass, a choice rooted more in the practicalities afforded by technology than anything else: lower cost, uniform consistency, and minimal unintentional imperfections. Besides, in the pre-internet age, he was constrained by the supplies available at local brick-and-mortar art stores.

By contrast, medieval artisans used handblown glass. It can be seen in some of the world's most intricate and breathtaking stained-glass windows, from the Cathedral of Notre-Dame's French-glass rose windows to the Blue Mosque's two-hundred-plus Venetian-glass windows. Glassblowing, though, can be a notoriously finicky enterprise, and regardless of the glassblower's skill, each fabricated sheet will differ from all preceding and succeeding sheets, containing individual imperfections both big and small. Yet it's these imperfections—the waves, striations, bubbles—that somehow enhance the natural beauty and character of each piece, providing texture and depth to Noah's wooden ark, the flowing robes of disciples and supplicants, and bouquet of blooming flowers reaching skyward from a vase.

While the modern manufacturing process creates greater consistency and minimizes imperfections, manufacturers still manage to introduce the illusion of the imperfections found in handblown glass, with each artist choosing the texture and appearance that evokes in the beholder, through more than imagery alone, the three-dimensional feel of water, flowers, clouds, clothes, leaves, and wood.

But no glass, whether handblown or manufactured, is free of all imperfections. Some may be superficial, others deep; some obvious, others imperceptible; yet imperfections they remain.

So it is that the truth about my father, like the man himself, is complicated. On the surface, things may have appeared perfect. The perfection was merely an illusion, though. Much like the glass he selected, scored, broke, arranged, and soldered, neither was my father free of brutal imperfections.

Then again, who among us is? Because, if the measure of a man or woman is limited to his or her positive attributes, then surely we must all fail the unforgiving measure of time.

★★★

Humans are complex, complicated, enigmatic. Each a kaleidoscope of virtues and flaws. What we see on the surface of another person represents a unique blend of disguise, half-truths, and the reflections of our own senses and projections of our own beliefs. As a result, we can never know the true, whole person.

Of course, recognizing this requires an appreciation for nuance. It requires accepting that good people sometimes do bad things and bad people sometimes do good things—that an individual's worth cannot necessarily be measured by an isolated act. To value a human according to little more than a backward-looking balance sheet of plusses and minuses leaves no room for redemption, for creating goodness and intangible worth.

I've generally been able to appreciate this nuance, to avoid myopically passing judgment. This explains why I never seriously considered working in the criminal justice system, a system that regularly defines an individual's holistic worth according to an isolated moment in time. Sure, in determining the just punishment for any crime, courts will consider the actor's history—past crimes, demographics and education, special skills and employment history, and, if provided, mental health reports and character letters—but this two-dimensional retelling barely scratches the surface, and I never felt comfortable being in a position to argue, based solely on some five- or ten- or twenty-page report, that *this* person, shaped by his or her unique experiences, deserved to be punished in *this* way or to *this* extent. I lacked the complete picture and, as such, could not rightfully pass judgment.

Except that passing judgment is what war demands, and passing judgment is what I did. Every time the commander asked about any legal objections, I judged. I judged whether the strike complied with the laws of war; whether the evidence supported a determination that *this* person belonged to an enemy group or had demonstrated hostility toward our forces; whether the strike might harm innocent bystanders, a phrase that implicitly excluded *this* person; and, ultimately, whether *this* person, the one whom we were targeting, deserved to die—or, more accurately, whether I had any legal objections to the commander so deciding—all for one act and without regard for the whole person.

That fragmentary judgment alone troubles me. But so, too, do the situations when my fragmentary judgment turned out to be wholly incorrect, or resulted in horribly unfortunate results, or permitted unabated recklessness that went unpunished. Because, in those situations, I directly participated in the acts that killed innocent people.

It's these acts—the innocent deaths caused by my failure to question the information about the targeted individual; to express concern with a rush to kill based on incomplete information; to advocate for patience as the motorcycle raced toward more populated centers; to push back against a subordinate commander's apparent thirst for death and unwarranted complaints about our "unreasonable delay" in approving strikes; to argue for thorough and impartial investigations into that commander's increasingly reckless conduct; to expose and open others' eyes to his team's blatantly falsified information; to prevent self-preservation from sweeping his actions under the rug; to take whatever steps were necessary to ensure someone held him accountable; to serve as a check on power; to err on the side of life— that haunt me, leaving me to question my "goodness." Whereas I could once compartmentalize my many wrongful acts and omissions, storing each in separate folders in a growing filing cabinet of memories where they might remain forever hidden and suppressed, unable to conspire and denied the opportunity to define me, that separation became untenable in late 2018. It was as though a tumultuous force had toppled the filing cabinet, showering me in the ticker tape of my once meticulously organized memories. And, as those memories settled into a disarrayed pile of imperfection, all nuance was lost. The inward-facing world became monochromatic, admitting no gradation, rigid in its classification: good or bad.

This monochromatic world is where I find myself when the snow falling over Virginia melts into rumination over my errors and imperfections, not just in Afghanistan but across my life.

Alexander Solzhenitsyn once wrote, "If only there were evil people somewhere insidiously committing evil deeds, and it were necessary only to separate them from the rest of us and destroy them. But the line dividing good and evil cuts through the heart of every human being. And who is willing to destroy a piece of his own heart?"

In my lifetime, I don't know that I ever truly examined myself, ever passed judgment on my worth. I simply wasn't willing to identify the piece of my heart that needed to be excised. But suddenly, in the aftermath of Afghanistan, I found myself on trial, standing naked before the harshest judge of all—me—as he pitilessly listed not only my failures in Afghanistan but also a lifetime of mistakes and falsehoods, flaws and frailties. Recalling, for example, the times when I lashed out, or acted carelessly, or behaved selfishly, or wished ill, or mocked and ridiculed others purely to boost my fragile self-esteem.

As the internal judge recounted the litany of offenses and prepared to render judgment on my heart, I began to question whether each offense had merely presaged the ones to come, whether I had been blind to who I had been all along, whether I even knew the real me; after all, when you are not the person you thought you were, you are not the person you are.

These acts and omissions became the mirror by which my imperfections were reflected. And what did that painfully efficient pedagogue named experience teach me? That, in Afghanistan, I caved to fear, to a desire for self-preservation, to a yearning to be liked. Though my spoken words professed integrity and courage, the mirror revealed my true unspoken character: a weak-kneed people-pleaser who often chose the self-interested path of least resistance. Except that, in Afghanistan, these character defects concerned life and death, resulting not in bruised egos or broken hearts repairable with time but in the premature and irreversible end to others' lives.

That mirror shattered into a thousand shards of glass with the realization that I had betrayed myself—my values and beliefs—during that deployment. Or had I? Hadn't I simply behaved consistent with my many preexisting imperfections and, as such, betrayed no personal mores? And if my bad acts merely reflected my true character, then the truth was just and only that: I was—am—a bad person. *This* is the nature of shame.

In the ensuing struggle to pick up those shards, to piece together a shattered self-worth, I cannot deny I've acted in ways that go against my values. But I also cannot ignore I've acted in ways consistent with them. There are parts of me I hate and parts I love, parts bad and parts good. It's just that I'm straining to identify any examples of the second. I want to discard the bad pieces, the imperfect pieces, but I'm not sure what, if anything, would remain. The sharp, stalking, elongated shadow of Afghanistan blots out any good. The true cost of conscious and conscience.

I have generally been forgiving of others, like my father. I accept that their imperfect acts rarely define their whole person. I am less forgiving of myself. There is no nuance there. A bad act makes a bad person.

My father, in the way parents are often more forgiving of their own children, would have been more compassionate in his assessment.

While I can't recall the impetus for his written affirmation, it likely stemmed from some mistake or perceived failure, maybe on the rifle range or physical fitness test, and communicated to him through the eyes of that harsh judge. Whatever the cause, my dad responded, attempting to silence the judge—"Quit being so critical of yourself."—before reminding me of *his* assessment, the most important assessment: "You are a great son and person."

Notwithstanding my father's impatience and anger, mood swings and misfires, I'd like to believe he would have oriented me to the bigger picture, identifying where the bad pieces fit into the larger image of my imperfect self, reminding me that those failures in Afghanistan, even though they yielded far greater consequences, do not define me as a person any more so than my many failures before or the many that will come; that these errors and flaws, mistakes and failures simply reflect basic human nature, making me no less good than any other flawed human on earth; that, in the end, all I could do was "keep on doing your best." And, for good measure, repeating, as he did nearly twenty years before, the most welcomed fatherly affirmation: "As I said before, you are a great son, becoming a great man."

In retrospect, perhaps his hobby was the perfect allegory. After all, my father knew imperfection firsthand.

I am human, deeply flawed. But I cannot allow the imperfect pieces to dictate my value. That's too simplistic. Those pieces are a part of who I was, who I am—and perhaps who I can become.

So maybe my imperfections can still create something beautiful, something inspiring, something good. Like an isolated snowflake, like a piece of glass—like my father.

11. People Pleasing

"Y ou may be satisfied, but I'm not."

For those who survive through to the final week, the culminating event in the Ranger Assessment and Selection Program is an interview with a board composed of two senior officers and two senior enlisted members. These four voting members determine whether an individual will be selected for service in the 75th Ranger Regiment.

It's intimidating, this experience. Like some interview in a detective novel, the candidate sits guarded and girded in a lone chair, sweating under the white-hot glare of the uncomfortable spotlight, while four seasoned Rangers pepper him or her with questions, scrutinizing every answer, every facial expression, every shift in body language. Few escape unscathed.

Up to that point, the board represented the worst experience in my life. Everything went downhill the moment I opened my mouth, a snowball rolling into an avalanche.

The board members began with a few peremptory questions, my answers eliciting blank stares or disapproving grunts, the minutes stretching an eternity. After this introductory misery, the board president turned to the subject-matter expert, a nonvoting member present during the boards for specialists, like lawyers, and granted him permission to question me.

The judge advocate read a prepared question from his computer: "You're deployed overseas and the task force commander wants to strike a target. Assume the proposed strike satisfies the laws of armed conflict. However, something about the strike does not sit right with you. What advice do you offer the task force commander?"

It was a softball question. *Thank God*, I thought. I knew the "correct" answer, or the one I believed most commanders would want to hear. I was determined to hit this one out of the park.

"So the proposed strike is against a military target, distinguishes between civilian objects and persons, is proportionate in that harm to civilian objects or persons is not excessive in relation to the military advantages to be gained, and the proposed weaponeering solution causes no unnecessary suffering?" I asked rhetorically in an effort to demonstrate my technical knowledge. "Then my gut feeling is irrelevant. My job is to provide the task force commander with legal advice, so I would tell him I have no legal objections. If the task force commander wants to know my personal opinion, then he can ask and I will tell him. Otherwise, it's not my place to offer commentary."

"That's correct," the judge advocate responded, turning to the board president. "I'm satisfied with that answer."

"You may be satisfied, but I'm not," the gruff Ranger colonel snarled.

Yikes. It wasn't a home run, sure, but I thought my answer was at least a double. The snowball gained momentum.

"Describe the most complex legal issue you've ever faced," the colonel pressed.

Still reeling from the colonel's dissatisfaction, I struggled to think of an example that would impress him. I had encountered few truly complex legal issues during my time in service, so I thought back to my time in private practice. "Off the top of my head," I couched, before offering what I considered to be a suitably complex issue.

He waved me off brusquely. "I don't think that's very complex." In his voice was agitation but also conceit.

And this was the moment when an already bad experience turned downright horrifying. As the colonel dismissed my example, I unconsciously smirked. The colonel, catching the expression, exploded.

"Did you see that?!" he said, turning to the other board members. "Did you see what he just did?!" His fellow board members nodded silently. I stared at him, a confused deer in headlights. My fellow judge advocate lowered his head, more in fear than shame. The avalanche that would sound my death knell.

He turned his fire on me. "Do you know what you just did?"

"No, sir."

"You don't even know what you did! You don't even know what you did!" he continued. "Do you know what 'hubris' means?"

"It's unearned, exaggerated self-confidence, sir."

"You have remarkable hubris. Do you know how I know?"

"No, sir."

"You can't even hide it on your face. Your face betrayed you. You're arrogant. You smirked when I said your example wasn't that complex. You know what, I'm done with you. You're dismissed."

With sprinting heart and shaking hands, I stood, saluted, and walked out the door. If time spent in the board was the ultimate arbiter of success, my paltry ten minutes under the spotlight signaled abject failure. *Well, I fucked that up. There's no way I'm getting selected*, I thought as I prepared for the long trip home with tail firmly between my legs.

I stood in the nondescript hallway, a hallway that reminded me of those in the various nursing homes where my father resided over the years, waiting to be called back in for the board's verdict. On the verge of achieving the job I most wanted in the military, I had stumbled over an infelicitous display of pride.

After a decade inside several minutes, the board summoned me. I strode—there's that pride again—to the middle of the room, saluted, and waited for the board president to instruct me to sit. He barely acknowledged me, returning my salute only half-heartedly. "Be seated," he said, still dismissive of my worth.

The colonel lectured me about ego. He spoke about pride. And he expressed grave concern about my ability to provide what the unit needed from its lawyer in a deployed environment. I sat there quietly, back rigid, hands flat on the tops of my thighs, not knowing whether to cry or hang my head.

Once he finished his excoriation, the board members announced their votes, one by one.

Somehow, despite my smirk, despite my hubris, the 75th Ranger Regiment selected me.

The vote was three to one.

★★★

In 1992, Vai Sikahema, a running back and return specialist for the Philadelphia Eagles, caught a punt from the New York Giants's Sean Landeta at his own thirteen-yard line. Sikahema sprinted toward the right sideline, cut upfield, and returned the ball untouched for a touchdown. After crossing the goal line, Sikahema ran to the thick protective padding wrapped around the base of the goal post and, like a prize fighter preparing for his next heavyweight bout, threw a few jabs and hooks on the makeshift punching bag before teammates mobbed him. Sikahema would later call it his *Rocky* impersonation, an ode to the blockbuster boxing franchise about another Philadelphian, Rocky Balboa.

A year later, on a crisp autumn Saturday morning, an eleven-year-old boy took a toss in his backfield, rounded the left corner and, with dew flicking from his cleats, sprinted down the sideline. That eleven-year-old boy had watched the 1992 Eagles game, seen Sikahema's punt return, and absorbed the Rocky-esque celebration. As he neared the goal line with not a single defender in reach, the little boy decided it was his moment to shine. High-stepping across the goal line, he ran to the protective padding of the goal post and threw a few jabs and hooks on the makeshift punching bag before teammates mobbed him.

That eleven-year-old boy was me.

Oh, the many lessons I learned from this unhappy memory. It had been my first touchdown. Seeing as I hadn't been there before, I didn't know how to act like I had. I didn't yet understand winning, or losing, with grace. Even worse, I had made the score about me, ignoring that none of it—breaking the line of scrimmage, the scamper down the sideline, the score, the Rocky-Sikahema routine—would have been possible without my teammates. But these poignant lessons, which I wouldn't begin to appreciate until years later, were overshadowed by a lesson learned in shame.

After the game, my father drove the short mile from the stadium to our home. A lonely drive. The kind of drive with no music, no speaking, the air between us thick, heavy. The kind of drive that sounded like a bad omen.

We spent the afternoon in the basement watching college football on the big-screen television. Seated in his upholstered recliner, my father was quiet—unusually so. I noticed his tight jaw and pursed lips. I felt stifled heat in his scowl. Yet none of these warning signs kept me from opening my mouth. I wanted to relive my glory. I wanted praise. I wanted him to fawn over my touchdown.

What I wanted was not to be received.

I started retelling the story of the touchdown in the desperate solicitation of a father's approval. But instead of approval, my thirst for a shower of compliments drew tear-inducing scorn, bricks replacing bouquets.

In that calm, lowered tone I found far worse than his violent explosions, my father retold the story from his viewpoint. Of how he jumped to his feet in excitement as I turned the corner and sprinted down the sideline past the defenders, of how he cheered my name loudly—and of how he sat down quietly in shame when I celebrated. Dad concluded his monologue, saving the worst for last: "I was *embarrassed* by you. I was *embarrassed* to be in those stands."

The searing prick deflated me, all eighty pounds of me melting into the puddle formed from the resulting tears. I sat wounded, blubbering and sniffling on the couch opposite him, trying to hide the effects of his words, wishing for the earth to open beneath me as he continued watching TV, ignoring the little boy who suddenly felt infinitesimally small, like an ant squashed under the foot of a giant. It was a lesson in humility, but more.

We never spoke of the touchdown or his ensuing embarrassment again. And while this is my earliest memory of tasting my father's shame and swallowing my own, there would be others: the time when I was failing math; the time when my supervisor called my father and suspended me for calling a co-worker "bitch"; or the time I cussed in front of my devoutly Christian choir director, using words I commonly heard at home, and experienced the unpleasant taste from a bar of soap by my father's hand, to name a few.

To one who pines for a parent's attention, affection, and approval, shame is easily internalized and not easily forgotten.

★★★

Understanding other humans—their experiences, motivations, insecurities, wants, and needs—can be challenging under the best of circumstances, even with those whom we know best. It's just that so much of our existence remains insular.

In making sense of my father, Alzheimer's adds an additional layer of complexity, preventing me from approaching the source for firsthand information, however skewed, shielded, or superficial his answers. My understanding, then, is bounded by my experiences and supplemented by the memories of others who, like me, perceived only fragments on the fabric of his life through their own shaded lenses. My father's identity will always be incomplete, unknowable.

But I can guess, with some measure of certainty.

My father cared what other people thought about him, of him. The perceptions of others became the mirror in which he evaluated his identity, his worth. When he didn't like what he saw, he simply changed his clothes. Like a chameleon of sorts.

Sure, he would have denied this if asked, keeping it buried in some crevice where not even he acknowledged the discontent. And sure, as with most things human, it was more complicated than this. Even so, I don't doubt its truth.

My suspicion is supported by the observations of an impressionable boy, many of which in retrospect suggest that what my father wanted to be versus what he was created a disunity in him, a crisis of identity equal parts professed authenticity and discomforting shame. And what were those observations? Well, for one, there was the grand brick home constructed on a large plat of land. Then there was the oversized pond built in the backyard; the Lincoln Continental that sat in the driveway collecting pollen; the Clark Griswold-inspired Christmas decorations that drew gawkers; the expensive dinners and overpriced bottles of wine; the yearly vacations at an extravagant rented Outer Banks beach house; the excessive quantity of gifts for his spouse, children, and grandchildren at Christmastime; the financial donations to the high school music department and other charities; and the basement renovations that provided the backdrop for his lavish alcohol-laced parties. Then there were his rebuffs to any suggestion that he resembled Danny DeVito (and also Dennis Franz), his desire to be seen as handsome lost in the comparison. Finally, there was his unstated preoccupation with upward mobility and status, with cultivating friends of higher social caste, and the adoption of the gaudy stereotyped fashion to project an ancestry he couldn't claim, complete with the gold chains and pinky ring.

These observations are just and only that, free of retrospective judgment. This is not some hypocritical critique. At some level, we all desire acceptance; we all want to be liked, esteemed even.

Nor am I suggesting my father's motivations weren't varied. Our actions rarely trace their source to singular or even binary motives. The yearly trips to the Outer Banks, for example, demonstrated his solidly middle-class bona fides but also, and perhaps above all, served the ends of fun and relaxation with the family he loved.

Maybe my suspicions are unfounded. I allow room for the possibility of error. Even so, I cannot help trying to delicately excavate his inner depths. I yearn to extract some deeper picture of this inscrutable man in order to understand him better, and through him, me. And in doing so, I cannot ignore the inescapable conclusion formed by the common thread running through these observations: some element of my father remained dissatisfied with who he was and who he was not—ever denying the one, ever striving for the other. This dissatisfaction seemed to leave him restless, as though he was chasing some elusive trophy of assuredness in the untouched yet ever-untouchable distance, hoping that by finding the right identity, he might find longer arms too.

All of which brings me back to shame. You see, this struggle with others' perceptions is one of pride and shame. Like it or not, external judgments can affect our identity. And, if we're not careful, these external judgments can become a prophecy unto themselves, the perception of others informing our perception of ourself, defining who we are as a person. In the positive, that's ultimately about pride—we're beautiful or intelligent or generous or wealthy; in the negative, that's ultimately about shame—we're ugly or dumb or selfish or poor. Over time and with enough practice, we internalize these perceptions. They become our own.

So just as the touchdown run wasn't about me, neither was my celebration. Not entirely. Yes, my father wanted to teach humility. Yes, he wanted to raise me well. But when I think about my father's words and his embarrassment in the context of these youthful observations, I realize that what concerned him equally so, if not more, was *his* image in the eyes of others. My father felt embarrassed then because of his underlying preoccupation with how others perceived him. It was as much about what my actions said about him as it was about the actions themselves. Other parents watched my celebration, other parents connected me to my father. Their perception of him in that moment—real or imagined, accurate or not—pushed against the edges of insecurity over his identity. My father gazed into the mirror and disliked what he saw, the child's foibles reflected on the father. And he felt shame.

I wonder what precipitated this preoccupation with external perception. Was this preoccupation something present in him from birth, or was it learned early as his developing brain connected receipt of affection to others' positive perceptions of him, a conditioned response spawned long before his infant mind became conscious of the connection? Or was it the result of something his father once said to him in a moment of parental embarrassment? Or was it the result of uncertainty brought about by the end of his first marriage? Or was it something else, or everything? Does the answer matter?

Looking back on his piercing criticism of me, I wonder whether that Saturday represents a defining moment in the starting point of my life. I internalized my father's words. His embarrassment became mine. I was desperate to never again see that ugly reflection in the mirror. In my own way, then, I began changing my clothes.

I hid behind people pleasing, a woolen garment woven from acceptable actions and behavior, positive attributes, and conflict avoidance. Beholden to the perceptions of others, namely those I loved, but not just, I placed their wants, needs, and feelings on a pedestal. I wanted to be liked not necessarily for the sake of being liked, but because the opposite—criticism, conflict, censure—inflamed the brooding negative self-talk. The garment of positive perceptions provided validation of my worth, helping to smother the flames yet, in a twist of irony, snuffing out my identity too.

The importance I accorded these external perceptions manifested in other ways. That dedication in school, the very same dedication my dad praised when he wrote, "I was always impressed how prepared and dedicated you were in school," was another form of people pleasing. Achievements and accolades, whether academic or otherwise, became impressive data points, raising my esteem in the eyes of others—and, by extension, my own.

Yet these accomplishments always felt hollow, meaningless, and short-lived. I derived little personal satisfaction from them. Part of this can be traced to my father's reaction to the touchdown celebration. At eleven, I didn't yet understand the distinction between acceptable and unacceptable forms of celebration, between nuance and rigidity. Instead, the lesson I learned was one of extremes: humility means never celebrating our accomplishments. Celebration became synonymous with gloating.

But more than that, my lack of personal satisfaction was an outgrowth of deriving validation from *out there*. As others' memories of the achievement fades, so do pride and self-worth. And that's the source of the emptiness. So I developed an addiction to achievements, chasing gold stars like an addict chases a high. Never satisfied; always restless. Incessantly looking ahead to the next goal, the next achievement, the next fix. Desperate to fill the void of self-confidence; each time left wanting.

My guess as to my father's identity, then, is an educated one. I know because I feel these things in me. A portion of my inheritance, the father's foibles reflected in the child.

★★★

I think often about that heaviest week in Afghanistan. If not every day, then most days. It haunts me like an unrelenting ghost, floating in and out of the present at whim. That's my life now: a life where past is present, and the future, the past.

Except the ghost no longer haunts alone. He's joined by others, far and near, who swirl—dipping, diving, menacing, and threatening to sweep me away. Ghosts born variously over a lifetime. Ghosts, like my father's embarrassment and the colonel's doubts.

In many ways, Afghanistan represents a defining moment in the midpoint of my life: a shift seismic in its nature yet one set in motion twenty-five years earlier before a warm fire in a cold room after a touchdown gone awry.

When the gruff colonel expressed dissatisfaction with my answers and erupted at my hubris, he noticed a deficiency in me that had escaped the other board members. Having witnessed countless Rangers come through the organization, he developed a sixth sense for those who couldn't withstand the rigors. He termed it "complexity," speaking about the complexity of issues underpinning the unit's mission. But was he? Because it seems to me his use of "complexity" carried far more weight than the word was meant to bear.

What the colonel perceived was my propensity for pleasing others, a propensity that foretold of severe consequences. The organization depended upon its lawyers, perhaps above all others, to give the hard answers in the most demanding environment. It was the complexity not of the mission or the legal issues but of human relationships, of remaining authentic, of staring into the face of impossibly hard questions with equally awful answers and having the courage to uphold nonnegotiable values without concern for the resulting social costs. He knew from experience that everyone, from a man to a woman, would encounter a scenario when someone suggested something that represented a bad idea, and that he or she would be forced to decide whether to speak up or stay silent. He knew a person whose ego, whose pride needed validation from others' perceptions would rarely make the correct decision. That is what he perceived in my softball answer and smirking litany of achievements. And did his assessment not prove accurate?

I had watched my father shape-shift over the course of a decade, two maybe. But where my father's focus on others' perceptions was a victimless crime, mine was not. My victims suffered the consequences of a disloyalty of authenticity. Because, as I examine the choices I made and didn't make that heaviest week, I see now that all of it derived, in an unbroken chain of events, from my need to please others. I needed an anodyne for what plagued my self-confidence. This meant betraying my authentic self to be the person others wanted me to be: a lawyer who said yes, who never strayed from his lane, who allowed them—us—to kill. Except, that's not what the team wanted.

This truth was lost on me, my identity so tied up in others' perceptions. I didn't speak up or speak out not because I didn't know the correct answer but because I couldn't handle the internal effects of external causes. I couldn't handle disappointment staring back at me in the mirror. So the choice for me in Afghanistan—that impossibly hard question with equally bad answers—became one between shame and shame. If I spoke up or spoke out, I faced the shame of my teammates' disappointment and anger; if I didn't, I faced my own. True to my propensity, I chose the latter. And that's what did me in, what broke me, what killed my victims and me. I had spent so long pretending that it took undeserving death for me to finally realize I no longer knew the real me. I wanted to like the reflection then; I hate the reflection now.

What I understand all too belatedly is what I wanted more than anything: to see my *father's* pride reflected in the mirror of my life.

Because it was his perception of me that mattered most. The people pleasing, the dogged pursuit of achievements—all of it was, above all else and at once, my desire to avoid disappointing him and a yearning for his approval, his love, his pride. And when my achievements didn't generate the gushing displays I expected, I chased the next star, my life becoming a series of attempts to find that one achievement that redeemed my mistakes and his disappointments, that induced bragging and praise, that forever cemented his pride in being my father. It was a fool's errand.

And what would Dad think now? Would he be ashamed of me again? I can guess, with some measure of certainty.

"I'm proud of you."

My father's pride, that emotional reaction to which I desired to be the object, was there all along. Like his love, rarely spoken but always present, always real. Hidden in the stolen sideways glances and bittersweet smiles; tasted in the heartfelt hugs and insistent embraces that felt something like release. My father didn't need me to please him, chase achievements, acquire wealth. All he needed me to do—all I needed to do—was be me. The real me.

Because my father was proud of me for an identity I couldn't change or fake, for who I was: his son.

And, in every way, that's all that matters.

12. Love Brings Us Home

I sit reminiscing at the edge of a wide, desolate river in Virginia, two full seasons after the snow. My father's been moved to a third nursing home now. He no longer paces, no longer moves, no longer opens his eyes. He just breathes. I can sense the end to his journey. Our journey.

The surrounding forest—dark, dense, mottled by autumn's splashes—amplifies the river's tympanic rumble as it cascades over the rocks impeding its path. I grab a handful of the spongy black soil and bring it to my nose, inhaling the earth's sweet perfume. I should be making camp, but embracing the solitude and listening to nature's requiem a bit longer seems more soothing.

I hear the whispering wind approach. It soughs through the trees, prematurely separating a handful of speckled leaves, robbing them of the chance to peak and burst forth in resplendent reds, oranges, and yellows. I watch as they dance their slow, final dance with the wind— twisting, turning, floating, fluttering, winding, wobbling—before, one by one, alighting on the surrounding surfaces.

One settles on an exposed rock on the precipice of a waterfall. The leaf reminds me of a man lying on his back, hands resting beneath his head, gazing in wonder at the thousands of tiny candles flickering against the cold black expanse. I accept the intimation and lie back in imitation. With the cold earth at my back, I feel the homesickness seep through me once again.

★★★

For as long as I can remember, there's been this constant indescribable tension between home and away, between the here and there, between the present and the future tearing at me. In adolescence, this manifested most in a need to escape the hamlet that buttressed the formative years of my youth.

That tiny town of two thousand or so inhabitants, located squarely in the former coal belt of Pennsylvania, offered little hope beyond a continuous cycle of immobility. With few exceptions, most of those inhabitants, like their forebearers, had lived within a roughly ten-mile radius their entire lives, seldom knowing different. Couples gave birth to children; those children attended the local school, grew into adults, worked local jobs offering little prospect for advancement, gave birth to a new generation; the cycle repeated on the seeds sowed by the new generation, and on and on in perpetuity, never to change, until it did. It was the sort of undiversified place where everyone knew everything about everyone—their secrets, fears, successes, failures—and where word spread faster than fire to a drought-stricken forest.

While this existence may have been fine for everyone else, it wasn't for me. I couldn't wait to leave. I couldn't subscribe to a lifetime living in what felt like a stagnant pond. I needed to make something of myself, to accomplish "great" things, whatever that meant. To do that, I had to get out, go somewhere special. As soon as possible, never to return.

I was searching in desperation for something. What exactly, I didn't know, but I was sure it was out *there* somewhere, waiting to be seized, molded, and possessed.

The Marine Corps reserves offered the first respite from the doldrums, a taste of what lay beyond on life's path, across the ocean of possibility surging to meet some distant horizon. Though I knew this taste would last only a few months before a ripple, barely a wave, would carry me home for college, this planned return to central Pennsylvania represented little more than a minor detour from the path toward a vision of life far removed from that stifling hamlet. I was dipping my toes into that ocean of possibility and touching the first Bimini stone, one that would eventually lead, by fate or happenstance, to Afghanistan and beyond. Yet a funny thing happened during that first dip of welcomed sea change: homesickness.

This homesickness would be a recurring theme in the letters exchanged by father and son that summer. At night, under starched white cotton sheets and a scratchy olive drab blanket on the top bunk of a squeaky metal frame, I'd gaze forlornly out the bay window, across the marsh, to cars crossing a bridge linking nearby Beaufort to Cat Island, thinking about home while envy and sadness coursed, longing to be a child in one of those cars, driving to some destination with Dad.

He did his best to abate the symptoms. "I don't think you ever get over being homesick throughout your life. There are too many good memories that you don't want to forget them. You feel that way because they are pleasant feelings compared to the tough time you're going through," Dad wrote. Two weeks later, he added: "I'm sorry to hear that the homesickness is still eating at you. Maybe it will let up soon. Don't be discouraged that it's still bothering you. They say home is where your heart is so it's understandable how you feel. You have compassion like I do."

But my dad's words, pored over through blurry vision, provided only temporary relief from the storm surge of emotions that pounded my shores relentlessly that summer. And when the relief wore off, I turned needy, begging for his affirmation, soliciting his reassurance that I was not alone in my misery. "Yes I want to hug you and see you so much it hurts," he assured me. "But I'm counting the days and each day is closer to seeing you. That's my motivation."

Eager to leave yet yearning to return—two desires at equal variance.

How could this be? I had wanted nothing more than to get out, to chart a new course, to avoid a circumscribed life long on monotony and short on joy. Now out, I wanted back in? What was my problem?

★★★

Lending truth to my dad's words, the homesickness never went away, continuing to plague me through the years like some incurable condition.

As with an autoimmune disease, the symptoms would come and go, as varied as the cause, at times presenting for me as nostalgia, at times as a sort of physical and metaphysical wanderlust, but always a pervasive discontent and agitating restlessness. And is this not also what homesickness is? An undefined, unquenchable wandering in search of that which brings spiritual peace?

So I wandered, searching—trying to get somewhere, never arriving. Wanting to discover not only new places but also a spiritual salve that might finally comfort me. In academics and my career, this led to hunting without for the missing within, chasing accomplishment after accomplishment in pursuit of external validation of my worth, rarely resting, always ravenous, never fulfilled; in the remainder, to travel. Underlying it all was some unidentifiable, unplaceable dissatisfaction. And it created friction in my marriage.

We had been young when we married, Marcela and I, unaware of the baggage we carried into the relationship, uncertain of our identities, unconscious of our insecurities. These would be challenges enough for any relationship. But then my father's diagnosis happened and my wandering worsened.

Yet we never spoke of its cause. We joined the Army and moved away from the home we had built as the chip in the windshield of our marriage went unattended, invisibly weakening the glass, waiting for a bump in the road that would create a spiderweb too large to ignore.

Afghanistan was that bump, hit at full speed. But it occurred after years spent ignoring the chip and weakening glass.

Marcela frequently commented on my restlessness, probing as to its cause while inwardly interpreting my discontent as unhappiness with her. It was a reasonable interpretation. Not because of its truth but because of my inability to diagnose the cause or find the curing words.

We discussed this topic on a fall trip to Vermont shortly after the deployment that changed everything. As we meandered along a gravel country road lined by picturesque red and orange and yellow leaves, we were strangely oblivious to the intense symbolism of autumn—the impermanence; the onset of cold, dark days; the growth through letting go and beginning anew; the invariable cycle of life—which underscored our reliving of memories, expressions of fear, and useless attempts to pinpoint the cause of our invisible decline, all against the backdrop of gentle rain pattering the leaves around us, nature's arresting tap-tap-tap marking the unstoppable passage of seconds, minutes, and hours. It was the sort of walk that reminded me of our beginning fourteen years earlier, of the hours spent on a rooftop in the French Quarter discussing physics and the Rwandan genocide and everything in between. And whether it was the rain, or the autumn allure, or the intimacy created by Marcela's generous heart and empathetic ears, it reminded me of why I loved her.

At one point during the conversation, Marcela offered a hypothesis for what caused our marriage to stagnate. "Sometimes I wonder if my general risk aversion pushed you away."

"What do you mean?" I asked.

"I wonder whether my conservative approach to life or hesitancy to take big risks created some resentment that slowly affected us."

I considered her hypothesis as we continued walking.

"But I think it was really something deeper than fears about logistics or taking risks. Like, you'd send me a listing for a cabin or talk about moving to another country, but those plans never seemed to include me. You never said 'we' or 'us.' It just felt like you were unhappy and trying to get away from me. So I would ask things like, 'Well, how will we afford this?' or 'What about the dogs? What will we do with them?' when really I was just afraid of losing you. And my fear is that, by holding on so tightly and shutting these things down, I actually added to your unhappiness and just pushed you away."

It was an unfair attempt to lay the blame at her own feet. Even so, I still think about her random musing.

I was dissatisfied. I was unfulfilled. I was restless. Marcela's focus on what ailed me often aimed at the objects of my desires, desires expressed though the articles about married couples who quit their jobs to travel the world, fanciful suggestions that we move to a foreign country, discussions about buying land and building a remote cabin.

Maybe these were gentle, subconscious prods to gauge her interest and spirit for adventure. Maybe my offhanded suggestions originated with a belated shift in perspective brought about by my father's diagnosis, a desire to make the most of a fugitive life by enjoying the present against the prospect of an unknown future. Maybe my father's diagnosis played no part in those suggestions. I don't know. But it was clear I was searching for something.

It's not that Marcela didn't share in my wanderlust; she did. We freely gave in to those mutual cravings, traveling extensively, sampling new food, new cultures, new language, and building pleasant and unpleasant memories with each. But Marcela also suffered from her own version of homesickness. It wasn't the traditional longing for home. It was the longing for *a* home. A sort of "home-absence" brought about by frequent military-induced moves. These moves left her craving a home base, a physical place we could call our own and return to from time to time for some much-needed grounding.

This physicality held less sway for me, taking a backseat to the sickness plaguing my soul. And my unwavering preoccupation with that transient, metaphysical, ever-elusive spiritual need, coupled with my inability to identify it, may have unknowingly precipitated our unraveling.

It wasn't necessarily Marcela's conservativeness, risk aversion, or insecurities. It was the *something else* calling me.

★★★

Oddly, I again find myself pulled back to the stifling hamlet I once yearned to escape. It's a consequence of the Sturm und Drang the experiences in Afghanistan brought to bear—the newest "tough time" in my life, to borrow my dad's words from many years ago.

It's similar to what I felt during boot camp, when eighteen-year-old me wanted to go home, or so that child thought. What exceeded my eighteen-year-old comprehension only became clear with a longer tail behind me.

What am I saying?

I don't want to go home. I never wanted to go home. Returning to that tiny town isn't—wasn't—what I desire. What I desire is an impossible return. A return to the way things were, to the me before everything was taken, to a time when the emptiness wasn't so outsize, when life was carefree and simple.

Just as during boot camp, I'm longing not for a place but a person.

So much of the former me is tied up in my father, bound to him in time and space in the placeless memories. Frozen in the past experiences of Afghanistan, I feel myself drawn to a more distant past, to the safety and comfort of the familiar, to him.

That was the superficial meaning of my dad's words to me during the "tough time" of boot camp. I felt homesick because I longed for those familiar comforts of home. I wanted a return to the freedom and insouciance lost when, in the wee hours of June 13, 2000, I stepped onto those infamous yellow footprints on Parris Island only to be greeted by screaming drill instructors who would make every decision for me over the next thirteen weeks.

But I would be remiss in not probing further. Because, beyond the platitudes, my father was attempting to communicate something more profound in his solacing words on homesickness. It just took me being empty to understand.

When Dad wrote of "good memories that you don't want to forget" and "pleasant feelings," he wasn't speaking about a physical location where memories are formed and comforts felt. It wasn't the familiar comfort of a place, it was the familiar comfort of love; he was speaking to the heart, he was speaking about love.

Those good memories and pleasant feelings originate in love—with love and from love—creating a familiarity that transcends time and space. When we're absent, when we're far removed from those familiar feelings, when we feel wander tugging at the contours of our soul, it's because we're craving that missing piece. We feel homesick because we feel un-whole. We feel hollow. *That* was the meaning buried deep within his words. My dad felt it too: "I get a hollow feeling when you're gone," he wrote.

We spend much of our lives searching outward for something that fills the emptiness inward. The condition may lay dormant, the symptoms may change, but the sickness never goes away. And when those symptoms reemerge, we search for the medicine that alleviates our newest emptiness.

That medicine is love. Whether from a father's reassurance that he misses you and counts the days until you return or from a romantic partner, it is love that supplies the missing piece that fills our emptiness; love that completes us; love that brings us home.

I think back to the conversation on September 16th, when I told Marcela that I loved her but was not *in love* with her, and wonder whether being in love is merely another marker of this emptiness fulfilled, a notion embodied in the proverb "absence makes the heart grow fonder." Because being in love replicates the pleasant feelings we attach to home, however few or many, instantly transporting us to a time and place when the missing piece wasn't so missing, when we felt safe and comfortable. When we locate that missing piece of our soul in someone else—well, it feels a lot like home.

Over time, we take that love for granted, and when it's gone, when it's absent, our souls begin to wander again, striving to recapture those good memories and pleasant feelings once more. We feel loveless, so we search anew for the missing piece, for that one thing that leaves us just a bit less hollow.

The cure is the opposite of the cause.

Marcela and I were both searching in our own ways for medicine to fill our emptiness, to supply the missing piece, to recapture those familiar feelings associated with our childhood homes. That was my father's point, poignant in its simplicity: it wasn't the place, per se, but the feelings associated with the place to which we feel drawn over and over again.

My wife labeled the object of her search "a home base." Although she may have been speaking about a physical place, she did so only as a stand-in—a metaphor for the true object of her search: a requited love that provided the missing piece of her soul. While I was looking for a home *out there*, Marcela was looking for a home in me.

Perhaps, like my father, she understood it best all along.

★★★

This newfound awareness comes to me riding on the wind soughing through the trees as I sit on the banks of that desolate river.

I'm still desperately searching for something. Except I'm not searching out there. I'm searching in here. For me. For who I am now. Because I'm lost. I'm hollow. Some *thing* is missing.

And with my father, another part too.

The missing piece is him, the wind whispers.

My father's deterioration has left me without a keystone, and the sickness I feel is the search for something that feels like his presence. I am, at bottom, homesick for Dad.

It's just that a homecoming no longer seems possible. We're both gone—Dad to Alzheimer's, me to war. So I am drawn to my home in that tiny town, the last place where I found Dad. It's an ill substitute for what I need.

I look up at the crescent moon waning, rising above the trees, its pale light glinting off the rushing water. The illuminated sliver of silver-gray lies at the bottom of the sphere, pushing back against its dark side. In a few days, darkness will replace all remaining light as the moon's cycle ends before starting over.

Something about that silent illuminated sliver gives off the appearance of downcast eyes, a celestial rendition of a modern-day emoji. It is as if the moon reflects the collective yearning for my father. And in that moon, I see him: his soft, tired, gloomy eyes, laboring under the weight of the surrounding darkness.

I remember something my dad told me once, long before he developed Alzheimer's and forgot me, during a different heavy bout of homesickness. "When you're lonely, when you miss home," he said, laying his hand on my shoulder, "look up into the night sky and remember we're looking at the same moon."

It felt corny then, and now. Except, as with his other consoling clichés and pacifying platitudes, phrases that had seemed almost meaningless at first only to later assume some deeper significance, this, too, had two tales.

Seeing the moon reminds me of my dad's presence even in his absence, his corny comfort forever etched on my heart. He was my constant, the planet to my moon, providing the gravitational pull that slung me around in orbit, allowing me to drift away before pulling me back. My home lived in him.

I am besieged by memories of him at every turn. Every day, every season surfaces bittersweet reminders of a life that now seems so distant as to be myth. But I am certain it was real. How could it not have been when something so simple as white sneakers and stretched tube socks, Frankie Valli and Smokey Robinson, Christmas lights and stained-glass windows, backyard ponds and weathered gazebos, pole vaulters and Danny DeVito, roller coasters and funnel cakes, clowns and lion tamers, marching bands and college football, forked flames and glowing embers, sticky ice cream on a warm summer night and piping coffee on a cold winter day, and the rumbling of distant thunder arouses a sentimental happiness that penetrates the numbness, however deciduous the happiness may be.

And that's when it dawns on me: that missing piece isn't missing. Because Dad is everywhere and in me: buried in the memories, the stories, the words—in the love that never dies.

I want a return not to the hearthstone of a town but to the hearthstone of the heart.

With this observation, I feel Dad close. A warmth slowly spreads through my body, and for a moment, I feel less hollow; the homesickness disappears. Dad can't forget me if I don't forget him. And so long as the moon continues to rise, I won't.

Maybe, just maybe, that some *thing* I've been searching for *out there* has been *in here* the entire time.

13. Love's Burden

Vermont did not repair our marriage, or beat back Afghanistan, or cure my father. Nor did Vermont resolve the homesickness—that search *out there*—that dogged our marriage for eleven years. All of that awaited our return.

But the realization that love fills our emptiness, brings us home, brought me one step closer. It provided the conclusion. I still needed to understand the cure; I still needed to understand love.

Marcela and I decided to separate after the move from Georgia to Virginia in 2019. Or rather: I decided, and Marcela acquiesced. Living separate from each other wasn't what she wanted.

Shortly after settling into my new apartment, I had a moment of panic. These moments had become increasingly common since returning from Afghanistan. But unlike most, which typically concerned Afghanistan or the feeling of going crazy, this moment of panic concerned my marriage.

"I'm scared," I texted anxiously. "I'm about to turn thirty-eight. I'm scared of making a decision I'll come to regret. I'm scared of having to start over again. I'm scared I'll never find someone else. I'm scared of being alone. Scared. I'm just scared."

My friend responded sympathetically. She had, after all, navigated her own divorce years earlier and understood, perhaps better than most, the raging inferno slowly and imperceptibly destroying me from the inside.

"You're scared—terrified—of hurting her too, and rightfully so," she diagnosed, before painfully reliving her own decision-making process. "Knowing he, too, was unhappy, that there was nothing in myself I could change enough to turn that around, and that he was willing to just sit by and pretend that everything was fine when it so clearly was not was, in large part, why I decided I had to go. I wanted to give him the opportunity to find true love and partnership every bit as much as I wanted those things for myself because I truly *did* care for him—"

Her words seemed foreign. My eyes focused myopically on each phrase—each word, each letter—in some desperate attempt to draw parallels and meaning. My heart quickened. Perspiration wept from my palms. The room began spinning faster and faster and faster as I read on.

And then came the sentence that stopped the spinning.

"I knew I was done the moment I knew I'd rejoice for him if he did find someone else."

★★★

In 1998, shortly after acquiring a driver's license and the welcomed emancipation it brings, I visited a local strip mall where a small, nondescript building bearing a bright red neon ARMED FORCES sign served as my community's gateway to military service. In this building, military recruiters representing the Army, Navy, Marine Corps, and Air Force attempted to persuade America's youth of the virtues of service to the nation or of the chance to escape the economic stagnation plaguing the once-vibrant blue-collar industrial centers scattered across rural America. For so many, the military offered an opportunity to escape the curse of perpetual mundanity and its progressive melancholy. I was a sixteen-year-old boy on a mission—a boy on the cusp of manhood who knew what he wanted. And all he needed was some bravado to stoke the youthful fervor. The office he planned to visit would lack none.

Haughty and cocksure, I flung open the door and moved with a purpose across the linoleum floor, ignoring the first office I encountered upon entering the building; that branch, the Air Force, aroused nothing in me. The remaining branches were arranged in zigzag fashion, and it was the door to the left, immediately past the Air Force, that represented the portal to my future.

I marched into the office to find the marine recruiter on a phone call. He acknowledged my presence and motioned toward the couch along the wall. More prey he needed to keep occupied until he finished his current meal.

I sat down and scanned my surroundings, fixating on the not-so-subtle symbolism of it all. The American flag hung behind me, reminding me that, above all else, I would serve and defend the nation. Marine posters adorned the walls, featuring men, all of whom were impossibly and ruggedly handsome, wearing stern, hard countenances, ready to do battle at a moment's notice. The posters required few words, conveying through imagery alone the corps's carefully crafted brand and professed reputation for badassery. Opposite the posters were ranks upon ranks of wallet-size boot camp photos. The photos, which featured fresh-faced, newly minted marines, stood testament to the countless local young men and women who preceded me. In their thousand-yard stares, I saw my future.

Honestly, I remember little of that first conversation with the recruiter. Surely he ended his call and we introduced ourselves; I most certainly expressed a desire to enlist. But what I do remember is leaving the office enamored, with bumper stickers in hand, drunk on giddiness and pride, and possessing an eagerness for some unearned and premature nostalgia. I had, after all, already envisioned a future where I'd be looking back at my boot camp photo on that same office wall.

Those emotions were all that was necessary. I didn't need the hard sell—the "best service" arguments or litany of benefits or myriad other talking points to which recruiters resort in getting a potential enlistee across the proverbial finish line. I wanted to be a marine, pure and simple. I wanted what I viewed, or thought society viewed, to be the true test of manhood. Any other perk was icing on the cake. Truth be told, I was a recruiter's wet dream.

The person for whom that hard sell would be reserved was my father. When I revealed my desire to enlist shortly thereafter, he pushed back. Hard.

He questioned my reasoning. He questioned how service would affect my dreams—or were they his dreams?—such as college and law school. I suppose my father thought this, too, shall pass; that it was just another fanciful, impetuous, emotionally driven whim of a boy searching for his identity, which, in retrospect, may well have been true. So he resorted to the long game, tolerating my incessant propagandizing and avoiding the subject altogether while laboring under the impression that, with time, he would prevail without ever needing to discuss the issue seriously.

My father was not anti-military service. Nor was he anti-war. He was just anti both for his youngest son.

In the late 1960s, my father learned he would be drafted into service. Rather than being forced into the Army, he'd enlisted in the Navy. His service was brief: shortly after reporting to boot camp, the Navy honorably discharged him for erroneous enlistment after learning of a preexisting injury to his wrist from pole vaulting in high school.

But my father, like many parents, distrusted recruiters. He frequently retold the story of reporting to the Military Entrance Processing Station, or MEPS, for his enlistment physical. When a sailor at MEPS asked my father to switch jobs to corpsman, my father refused, noting he had enlisted to serve as a journalist. The sailor burst into laughter. Maybe my father's trust issues began there.

Beyond distrust, my father wanted what he saw as a "better" life than the military for his son. For him, this meant college, law school, and greater financial security. At least this was my perception, and source of great frustration, at the time. Only years later would I realize that the source of his reluctance and obstinacy was something far deeper, more primal.

I couldn't enlist before my seventeenth birthday, and only then with my parents' permission, so I had approximately one year to weaken his resolve and win his acquiescence.

I was relentless.

So was my father.

Intent on following this dream, I approached these skirmishes as one might approach a debate. I identified what I believed to be his chief objection, namely that service would derail my future. My gut told me he feared I would never complete college, let alone law school, after enlisting. This fear further acceded to a slippery slope of undesirable fates, such as a post-service future spent working low-wage jobs just to make ends meet. It was not the future my father wanted for any of his children, let alone his youngest.

By anticipating his chief objection, I could prepare counterarguments that would rebut these fears. I laid out my intent and plan in great detail, providing a thorough timeline supported by evidence (in the form of recruiting brochures, of course). I would serve in the reserves. Once I completed initial training, I would return home to attend college; at most, I would miss one semester. Then, during college, I would participate in a marine officer training program and attend two six-week summer training programs at Officer Candidate School. Then, once I sat for the Law School Admission Test and gained admission to a law school, I would switch over into the law option, which would delay my commissioning until after graduation. Then, once I commissioned, I would begin service as a judge advocate in the Marine Corps. I had everything mapped out. The plan was solid, reasoned, and well argued.

My "opponent" was not convinced.

In the summer of 1998, my father had a few friends over to our home for a cookout. Among the guests that day was his best friend, Jimmy.

Jimmy had served as a marine during the Vietnam War. His experience, like that of many other Vietnam-era veterans, had a lasting and in some ways profoundly negative impact, one that my father witnessed dogging Jimmy over the years. As my father manned the grill, Jimmy began grilling me about the desire to enlist in the marines.

It was an ambush, but I was prepared to repel the assault. *Volley, counter-volley, volley, counter-volley.* By this point, I had restated my plan so many times that it rolled off my tongue like a well-rehearsed speech. Jimmy listened patiently before re-engaging.

Perhaps recognizing the almost certain failure with this direct approach, Jimmy turned to indirect fire. He spoke about what to expect at boot camp and in service and the hardness of it all in an attempt to strike deep within my mind, stoking fears and insecurities while playing to stereotyped generational apathy. If my father had intended for Jimmy's stories to scare me, his plan didn't work. If anything, Jimmy's stories contained an undercurrent of sentimentalism that only fed my hunger.

I'm not sure what transpired between my father and Jimmy after that conversation by the grill in our backyard. I don't know whether my father had planned the ambush. I don't know whether Jimmy advocated on my behalf behind the scenes. I don't even know whether the two discussed the subject at all.

But, in May 1999, my father signed the enlistment papers.

★★★

This wasn't the first battle we'd wage, nor would it be the last. His vocal opposition to my plans and dreams and desires would be repeated many times over the years. Sometimes the opposition would reveal my father's incongruity; for example, his response to my decision to attend law school in New Orleans: "New Orleans?! It's a war zone down there!" (Never mind the inconvenient truth of his annual trips to the Big Easy where he got smashed with friends on Bourbon Street.) At other times, it exposed his impetuousness; for example, his response to my plans to propose to Marcela: "Why?!" (Even though he thought the world of her.)

When I was a teenager, my father's opposition frustrated the shit out of me. To quote the immortal words of two of the twentieth century's great philosophers, DJ Jazzy Jeff and the Fresh Prince, "Parents Just

Don't Understand." Because in revealing my plans and dreams and desires, what I wanted more than anything was my dad's approval and support. Instead, what I felt was his rejection.

Over time, the frustration with his opposition dissipated, replaced instead by rolled eyes or a casual dismissiveness of his opinions. I knew better, after all. But like humidity after a passing afternoon shower, that palpable feeling of rejection hung heavy in the air between us. *Parents just don't understand.*

Except my father did. Just not in the ways that I understood.

Sure, there were the standard reasons for my father's obstinacy. He wanted me to make smart choices and to consider the consequences of my actions before leaping. He wanted the best for me and to protect me from ill-advised decisions. "Don't rush into anything too fast," he cautioned during boot camp. What I realized only years later, however, is that his obstinacy represented something far more basal than prudence. It wasn't disapproval of the decision to enlist, or to attend a law school in New Orleans, or to propose marriage to a beautiful woman my father was expressing in those moments; the decisions themselves were largely irrelevant emotional fodder. Rather, it was a reaction to what those decisions represented.

You see, my father's obstinacy was fear cloaked in wisdom's clothes. Here was his youngest son and last remaining child, and whose adult decisions—to enlist, to move to New Orleans, to marry—evidenced a gradually encroaching divergence in the overlapping lives of father and son. It was the allegory, and not the decisions themselves, that set the stage for a clash between fatherly love and fear, between holding on and letting go. Because my father didn't want to let go, didn't want to lose his youngest child, didn't want to say goodbye. He wasn't ready. He wasn't ready to accept the rapidly approaching closing chapter of his life. He wasn't ready to live in my shadows. So he held fast, tight to the last remaining invisible thread connecting father and son, desperate to prevent its natural disintegration, all the while reluctantly accepting his powerlessness over the wild winds of fate. Resigned to this uncomfortable reality, my father ultimately yielded, relinquishing control and permitting me to exercise free will, whether or not this will represented wisdom or folly in his eyes, but not before first putting up some fight. It took me years to understand the masks my father wore to hide his emotions. But I understand now.

I recall few instances from my childhood when my dad outwardly displayed affection or uttered an "I love you." It simply wasn't a common household phrase. Even when I moved away from home, the "I love yous" at the end of our phone conversations felt awkward, uncomfortable, and stilted. This was not his preferred manner for communicating his love. What I appreciate now, however, is that in these moments, when Dad fought me or pushed back on my choices, he wasn't voicing disapproval or rejection or dismissiveness. Dad was voicing his love. The purest expression of love, in fact: love at once selfish and selfless.

I doubt my father thought about his reactions in this way, as allegory for the nature of love. But what he did not understand consciously, he understood intuitively: love carries a heavy burden; the selfish pleasure and joy we derive from love must, in every case, yield to the pleasure and joy experienced by our beloved.

In his spontaneous reactions, my father betrayed his selfish desires, seeking to preserve the familiar, the comfortable, and the status quo. When the time for spontaneity waned, selflessness took hold. This is why, with the singular exception of my enlistment, his opposition always remained tepid, short-lived. Selfishly, my father didn't want to let go, but selflessly, he knew he had no choice. And so he did. For my father, selflessness always prevailed.

It was in his silent reluctance to let go that my dad said, "I love you, Drake" loudest.

★★★

It's these memories of my father's resistance and this newfound understanding of his behavior that come to me unannounced, arriving even before I have time to understand, the way a particular song arouses the butterflies of a first kiss or surfaces frivolous details from some distant trip to the beach. The sentiment expressed in my friend's text—"I knew I was done the moment I knew I'd rejoice for him if he did find someone else."—wasn't new. It was just suddenly obvious. As though by shaking loose these memories, my friend helped clear the way for the connection to take hold, for me to understand what we must willingly relinquish to love—for love.

For years, I rolled my eyes and dismissed my father's emotional reactions to my life choices. Now, on the precipice of a new chapter in my life, I chafe at my shortsightedness, the lack of grace in my judgment. I know far less than I thought.

And if my dad could speak, what might he say? Would he remove his mask, embrace me, explain the burden that love requires me to bear?

Because I'm paralyzed. I'm paralyzed between placating love's selfish impulses and heeding its selfless burden. On the one hand, fear grips me: fear of the unknown, of being alone, of having to begin anew, of losing a love that, quite honestly, is far better than I deserve. The fear that once masqueraded as wisdom in my father's reactions now underlies my own reluctance to let Marcela go.

On the other hand, I admit love's burden, a burden that requires me to set aside my own selfish desires for Marcela's happiness. Sure, part of what paralyzes me is the desire to avoid causing the pain and heartbreak I know will surely accompany the decision to let go. But even that statement betrays selfish desires; after all, I'm merely seeking to avoid my own discomfort. No, love requires *I* suffer that discomfort and pain for Marcela and for me, so that once her pain and anguish and grief and heartbreak subside, her happiness may finally and fully blossom. Only then will I have truly borne the burden of love.

In those moments when married couples share their deepest insecurities, those moments of intimacy that stitch a roommate into a spouse, Marcela would listen while I voiced concerns about certain career choices or shared regrets. Many times, these moments focused on the material trappings of a rich life—how leaving the law firm for the Army would mean a financial hit, with fewer trips abroad, fewer possessions, and fewer gifts. But they also touched upon the residual guilt over how military service impacted her life—the effect of frequent moves on her social network, the stress from a need for dual income but an employer reluctant to permit telework, her inability to practice law in a new jurisdiction without taking another bar exam, the career stagnation, and so on.

Yet none of this seemed to matter, except to me. Because, in those moments of intimacy, Marcela—that beautiful, loving, compassionate woman—would take my hand and reiterate that none of that mattered. She didn't need the large house, fancy car, expensive jewelry, or lavish trips. She didn't need the lucrative or high-profile career. What she needed, what she wanted, what she desired more than anything—was love.

And I want that for Marcela, I genuinely do. I want her to experience happiness, to live a fulfilling life, to find the love she craves, needs, and deserves. This requires me to let go, to grant her release, to be the one who now watches in agony as the invisible thread connecting us pulls taut and finally gives way. At the same time, I fear my incapacity for grieving the loss of her twice—once now and once when she finds someone else, with the grief of the second eclipsing the first.

Would I rejoice for Marcela if she found someone else? I don't know. Maybe? Perhaps not now, not yet. I'm just not ready. Selfishness still clings to me.

My dad explained the burden of love in his own way during boot camp, a hard lesson learned in the experiences one amasses willingly and unwillingly over a long, bittersweet life: "Father's Day wasn't the same without you here, and it was difficult. Now don't feel bad, I know you are doing what you want to do and I'm proud of you. I want you to be happy. Someday you will be a father and you will understand how I feel."

I finally understand. I understand that, someday, the time for letting go may arrive, when my retreat into Marcela's shadows will become necessary, when I must step aside. Why? Because I want Marcela to be happy.

And because Dad taught me that it's in the act of letting go that love unspoken speaks loudest.

14. On the Path to Finding Peace

The alarm wakes me mid-dream. Stirring, stuck somewhere between the dream's final act and conscious thought, I reach for the phone.

Fourteen months have passed since I returned home, four since Marcela and I separated, and I'm on vacation outside Mount Hood, Oregon, as far away from Afghanistan as possible. Yet everything feels eerily similar. Another night passes, another day breaks, and still I attempt to reclaim the silence.

It's early, too early. Two thirty a.m.? Three a.m.? I'm not sure. It's some ungodly hour. Far too early to rise while on a self-imposed break from reality and responsibilities, from the pain and guilt and depression and numbness that, far from fading, grow more and more insufferable. Besides, the bed seems content bearing my weary body.

I need to break free from the bed's warm embrace, though. Given all my struggles to do anything other than withdraw entirely from the world, I need to follow through with plans to get out and into the wild. I need to feel something that can provide respite, peace—even if that respite is temporary, that peace fleeting.

As I lay swathed in the sheets and comforter, the fog from the mid-dream jolt begins to lift, and my senses slowly return. Smell first: the slightly dank, musty smell of the cabin. Then touch: the feel of flannel sheets against my skin; the weight of my head supported by the pillow, body by the mattress; the recognition of my fingers, hands, toes, and feet. Then sound: the stillness found only in the dormant hush of night.

I stretch my somnolent body and blink into the darkness for a moment. An ambient chill fills the cabin and brushes my exposed head, the fire in the wood-burning stove long ago extinguished from a want of food. I anticipate the cold shock once I toss the sheets and comforter aside and scramble to get dressed before the chill saps all residual heat from my body. Except, for whatever reason, I don't. Instead, after tossing the sheets and comforter aside and placing my feet firmly on the uneven wooden floor, I pause, allowing the chill and heat to pass fluidly through my skin, equalizing the temperature between air and body in this early-morning dance with osmosis.

I stagger—quietly, carefully, so as not to disturb the stillness that is the night's province—to the living room where I had laid my clothes the night before. Even night, though, must surrender stillness to a new day's bustle. And so I apologize, before flicking on the cabin's interior lights.

Each movement removes an ounce of possibility, making turning back less and less likely, though still not impossible. Squinting hard to allow my pupils to adjust, I take the next steps, mechanically dressing myself as my brain attends to the checklist of items for the hike. *Headlamp. Gloves. Forest pass. Phone. Directions to the trailhead. Keys. Water.* My check complete, I flick off the lights and plunge back into the darkness.

Once outside the cabin, I lock the door using the light from my phone. A gentle rain falls, and I spend a few seconds debating whether to go back inside for a rain jacket. But I fear rationalizing reclusion, so I open the car door instead.

The rental car creeps down the single-lane gravel road that leads from the cabin to the abutting four-lane highway, its headlights stuttering to and fro with the ruts, causing only spasmodic illumination of imposing trees and phantom shadows. Given the hour, the traffic surprises me. Leaving the unpaved road, I reach for the radio, turn it off, and listen to the high-pitched rev of the engine accelerating before shifting into the next gear, the wiper blades thump-thumping back and forth, and the splashing of tires from passing cars as they rotate and grip the wet asphalt.

Soon, I am turning off the highway onto a narrow, winding two-lane road, hugging a bend to the right, then left, then right again, before bearing straight. There's a light bobbing on the opposite side. Speeding past, I register the runner. *She's up really fucking early for a run,* I think in admiration. Then: *Why am I doing this? I'd rather be in bed.* But I keep driving, less a conscious decision and more basic inertia. It just seems easier to keep going somewhere.

Arriving at the forest clearing that serves as a parking lot, I find myself alone. No cars, no people, no life. I sit there in silence for a moment, steeling myself. *No turning back now,* I offer persuasively.

The soft opaque glow from the center dome light illuminates the interior, a solitary glowing orb spilling into the rich surrounding blackness. I emerge from the glow and submit to the darkness once more.

The pleasant earthly mixture of pine needles, wet soil, and decaying leaves fills my nostrils. I stand motionless, inhaling the forest, the darkness, the tranquility. The rain has tapered, turning into a soft mist that floats gracefully, the microscopic droplets seeming to hover in the air before condensing on my hair and exposed skin. Switching on the headlamp, I locate the trailhead and follow the edge of light into nothingness.

The trail climbs arduously to a subalpine lake four miles or so above the trailhead. The hope is to catch a view of Mount Hood reflected on the lake's surface at sunrise, but the weather seems intent on conspiring against hope. With dampened spirits, standing at the threshold of this unknown path, I start walking. Might as well, after all; I'm already here.

Climbing relentlessly up and up and up toward the heavens as though the pass follows the distinctive pitch of a ski chalet's roof, I am unable to see the landscape beyond the headlamp's outstretched yellow cone. I try to imagine how different the trail will appear after daybreak and during the descent. From the limited illumination, I can make out trees immediately to my flanks but little beyond. I can also hear the rush of water cascading over rocks to the right. I peer over the edge, focusing my headlight on the source of the noise, and smile slightly as the beam reflects off the turbulent tumbling water below. *Things hidden by darkness visible in the light, shifts in perspective.* I shut out the thoughts that a bear or mountain cat could be among those things lurking, hidden by the darkness.

After approximately an hour, the trail levels out into a rolling heartbeat, falsely suggesting I've reached the pinnacle. I stop, expecting to see a clearing or at least an abyss into which the beam from the headlamp disappears, something that indicates, "Here, water clings to territory by force against an encroaching forest, yet trees stand in every direction." *Where the fuck is the lake?*

I ramble along as the trail arcs around to the left, hell-bent on finding the lake before the approaching first light. By my calculations, I have fifteen minutes or so before the earth's rotation brings about another inevitable dawn and with it, a new day, a new wasted opportunity, a similar dread. *The lake must be here, but where? How?* The arc continues. The aimless wandering continues.

Upon crossing a small stream covered in a thin crust of ice that splinters under my weight, I notice a clearing to the left through some trees. *Fuck yes!* I turn into the clearing as the soft pine needle carpet gives way to the delicate crunch of permafrost underfoot, the result of frigid nights and marshy terra at the lake's outermost edge.

I scan the lake using my headlamp. Passing from left to right, I catch something. I scan back to the left, setting the long tunnel from my headlamp upon an exposed fallen tree jutting out into a lake. Nature's pier. An invitation for respite. The perfect place for solitude and quiet reflection.

I step gingerly from the frozen earth onto the smooth, slick trunk. A translucent sheet of ice coats the water's surface not more than twelve inches below me, the ice clutching to the tree's rough, barky edges. The precarious traction, coupled with hollow darkness and balance hindered by inadequate sleep, concerns me. So I crouch slightly, using my hands for balance as I traverse the trunk's length out into the water. "I'm going to fall into this lake," I say to no one, with the sort of anxious chuckle that serves to expel fear from the body. Fortunately, I don't.

Reaching the spot I think will offer an unsurpassed view, I turn to face the direction of the sun's rise and lower onto the trunk. I turn off the headlamp and sit in the darkness. The trunk's icy surface delightfully seeps through my hiking pants; I, exchanging my heat and it, its cold. More osmosis.

The surrounding evergreens appear silhouetted against a cetacean blue sky, the earliest signs of the earth's rotation nearing twilight. No matter in which direction I gaze, all I can see in this impenetrable darkness are these silhouettes against the pre-dawn sky.

My heart rate begins to subside and my breathing becomes less labored. And what I notice most is what the increasing calm allows me to hear: nothing. Complete, utter silence. No wind, no animals, no rustling in the brush or pines. It is as though I had disturbed nature, and nature, naturally cautious of intruders, had fallen silent, warily examining my intentions. It was a silence so still, so total that I could hear the blood circulating in my ears; a silence so still, so total that I begin to question whether I had lost my hearing; a silence so still, so total that it cannot be described as anything but "nothingness."

Marveling at the surrounding silence, I feel the tension in my body dissipate, releasing more and more with each exhale. I relax. And slowly, as it realizes I lack any impure intentions, so, too, does nature. At first, I hear only sporadic water droplets pelting the forest floor, the natural consequence of their weight becoming more than any individual leaf can bear. Then, as the sky slowly and imperceptibly shifts from cetacean to midnight, midnight to oxford blue, the first chirrups of unseen birds arrive, their songs beckoning a new day, proving that life has sprung anew.

I lose myself in the splendor of the music, time becoming nonexistent. Their airy calls fill the wild amphitheater, drifting from the trees and floating effortlessly above the calm water, an untamed operatic aria in surround sound. There will be no encore, though, for when their songs conclude, the birds relinquish the stage.

No sooner had the birds concluded their song than I hear a splash at the far end of the lake. And shortly thereafter, another. Then another. I look toward the origin of the sounds in an attempt to identify their creator. *Fish? No, it can't be. Fish aren't jumping out of the water, you idiot. Maybe turtles sliding from their rocks into the lake? Not unless they're doing cannonballs like Dad in the pool.*

As cooler air descends, the splashes continue, followed by the sound of water being displaced, as though some unseen force is dragging its hand through the lake, like a woman gently tracing the soapy surface of a warm bath. *It must be ducks or geese. But why can't I see them? Why don't I hear any quacking or honking? Geese are known hecklers!* Watching and listening as the earth's rotation continues, light gradually replacing darkness.

More splashes. Except now, in the faint pre-dawn light, I can see an animal moving through the water in the distance, its movements betrayed by the resulting wake. *It's the Pacific Northwest Loch Ness monster!* Patiently I wait, following the animal as it winds casually through the water, a round bump breaking the surface, exposed, gliding from the far bank to the middle and back again, each time moving closer to my perch, occasionally stopping to let out grunts and snorts.

Now a similar sound comes from the left too. I turn my head and squint. *Otters!* Their tiny wakes, which now ripple and lap at the icy edges of this suspended log, carry an excitement that somehow pricks my numbness.

I can see three or four moving about on a half-submerged log a short distance from the lake's edge. I watch in wonderment as they go about their morning routines: playing, grooming, hunting. If the otters notice me, they seem content to indulge my voyeuristic desires from a healthy distance.

And in that moment, the simplest, most remarkable thing happens. I smile. Not a feigned smile, like one given to a passing greeter, nor an insincere smile, like one designed to fool the body into a positive mindset. Just a simple, unadorned, innocent smile. A smile that begins with the slightest curl at the corner of the lips and pulls at the corner of the eyes. A smile that's unstoppable, unconscious, unnoticed until it's too late to neutralize. A smile that evinces genuine, unbridled happiness.

The sky continues to lighten as I remain lost in voyeurism, unmasking the lake and surrounding forest's grandeur in the process. Evergreen forest rings the lake, its glassy surface broken only by the playful otters.

Immersed in this sanctuary of solitude, I look toward the mountain for the first time. Though the mist has floated away, clouds blanket the sky, weighing down the sullenness I'm unable to shake. I fear the mountain will remain hidden, that I'll be deprived of the view I've craved for so long.

Just as all hope begins to fade, the sun begins peeking above the horizon like Kilroy's big nose peeking above the wall. Though the surrounding mountains obscure the sun's brilliance, the reflection of its rays create a rainbow of colors so vivid that even my colorblindness can't disguise the opalescent display. The sky turns purple as a slight pink begins mixing with the lightening blue on the universe's palette; then, a brushstroke of lilac and a palette knife of honey.

Suddenly, I begin to perceive the outline of a mountain rising above the tree line on the far shore, its dark features powering through, penetrating the translucent clouds illuminated by the rising sun. *Maybe this will happen. Be patient.* I wait; the colors continue to mix and the otters play and the birds sing and the forest comes alive.

The clouds begin shifting, unveiling tantalizingly more of the imposing mountain's stately features. *A parting of the sea of clouds and fog.* As if reaching through a gap in the clouds, the sun bathes the mountain's slope in gold, exposing its hard black rock and snow-filled crevices. The clouds continue: shifting, mutating, separating ever more until—finally—a near-unobstructed view of the mountain.

I lower my eyes and stare at the lake's surface, not an otter's wake in sight, as though they've suspended gaiety to enjoy nature's majestic spectacle. And in that undisturbed surface, I admire the picturesque reflection of warm colors and clouds and mountains and trees while remembering something Dad once wrote to me: "Life is full of surprises, Drake, some are good and some are bad."

In the reflection, I catch a glimpse of myself and notice a smile. That simple, unadorned, innocent smile has returned. For the first time in a long time, I feel happiness, peace.

★★★

My love of hiking didn't form until well into adulthood. Hiking wasn't something I did frequently with my father, or anyone. But my earliest memory of hiking, and likely my first ever hike, occurred shortly after my mother and father separated for the last time.

The trail in central Pennsylvania that my father chose survives even to this day. Beginning in a northeasterly direction, it follows rolling terrain on a wide crushed-gravel path before turning east and then southeast. The trail slowly and gently narrows, funneling hikers onto the rocky, though nontechnical, single track that climbs a few hundred feet. Ferns flank the well-marked trail, reaching out to brush the shoulders of hikers, who trek for less than a mile through a dense forest of eastern hemlock, black cherry, red maple, and white oak.

At the top, hikers reach a well-known Native American lookout. The rocky outcrop faces north, providing a panoramic view of the sleepy town below and soft mountains rising in the distance. Nearby, mossy monoliths rise from the earth like blunted daggers, stone giants amid aging trees, silent testaments to two industries that supported Pennsylvania's early growth.

From that outcrop, the trail loops back around and concludes with a short southwardly descent to the trailhead and parking lot.

Thirty years removed, the trail seems rather unimpressive and undemanding. But to a little boy with no outdoor experience, the hike probably seemed at once exhilarating and daunting.

I've retold the story of this hike many times yet remember little about the experience. I don't remember the drive or the type of car my father owned. I don't remember the hike. I don't remember the view from the lookout. I don't remember if we took breaks. I don't remember exploring. I don't remember if my father and I talked during the hike, or about what. I don't remember the season, the weather, or my age.

What I do remember is the descent. The fear, the terror, the pain. The crying and screaming and running, and my father running, and my father picking me up and running.

Because on our descent, I stepped on a yellow-jacket nest.

The mosh pit of bees slammed into us from every side, every angle. Just when we thought we'd outrun them, I'd get stung again—and again—and again. Endlessly. It seemed like an eternity before we reached the car. My first experience with the shifting sense of time.

My father put me in the backseat and jumped behind the wheel. As he started the car, I'm sure Dad said something to the effect of, "It will be okay. You're going to be okay," almost foreshadowing what he would write years later, "God will take care of you." Then I'd get stung again by a hitchhiking yellow jacket hidden somewhere in my clothes. I cried body-heaving cries as he drove the thirty minutes to the nearest emergency room.

My most vivid memory of the emergency room is lying on a gurney, the shafts of my blonde hair forming a matted and tangled mass bee grave, and lifting my head to view the remains of unburied bees against the sterile white medical pillow. We had each been stung more than a hundred times by the aggressive defenders.

My father fared worse. His body responded poorly to the poison. His throat began to swell, breathing became more difficult, medical staff swung into action. The staff ultimately decided to keep him overnight for observation.

That night, my stepmother and I visited him in the hospital. It was the first time I had seen my father in a hospital bed, a herald of things to come later in life. I felt scared and, even worse, guilty—guilty that I had caused his suffering. If only I had never asked to go on that hike; if only I had been more careful on our descent; if only and only if. Another example of that child's sensitivity to his dad's emotions, and fear of his dad's rejection.

I can still picture that hospital room. My dad lay on a foam mattress, all but the form of his legs concealed by a sterile white sheet. The bed abutted a bay window overlooking the parking lot, and the black night and sharp lights worked to create a mirroring effect. I remember staring at him through the reflection: a boy, watching a boy, watching his dad from the periphery, trying to put distance between the dad's condition and the boy's pain, searching for something that might soften reality and make it all more palatable.

I broke from the reflection and turned back to my dad. He seemed in good spirits. Not the characteristically jovial man I knew, but good spirits still. Yet it all felt forced. His expression seemed distorted by emotional exhaustion and pain, and in Dad's eyes I saw that look of someone suddenly struck by the fear of the unknown. I suspect he sensed my fear and guilt, doing his best to dispel the one and assuage the other. But this was my dad, that vibrant forty-two-year-old man, clothed in an open-backed hospital gown, lying on a gurney-like hospital bed, and quite clearly in pain. His feeble words couldn't compete with those powerful images.

My father recovered quickly, and the doctor discharged him the following day. But I never forgot those images of fear, that feeling of guilt.

And we never went on another hike.

These days, in the lengthening shadow of my father's diagnosis, the memory of this experience brings to the forefront of my consciousness unwelcome images of the untold visits when my father and I did nothing but pace the second-floor hallway of his nursing home. Looking back, I suppose this was—in some cruel, heartless, ironic bookend to life—the only hiking we'd ever share again.

I try to be grateful, though: at least there were no bees.

★★★

The clouds materialize, a shroud of fog descends, and the reflection fades. As the sun backlights the clouds in ambers, oranges, and raspberries and all but the mountain's lower reaches disappear, I thank God for parting the clouds just long enough for me to experience this spectacle and for the tantalizingly brief moment of peace. I stand up on the log, inch my way down its length, and walk back into the forest. The otters are playing again.

I continue along the path ringing the lake before beginning the descent to the trailhead. Though I am on the downside now and the return will be far quicker, I take my time, discovering all I had missed during the climb in the dark. Everything seems new now.

The trail drops off precipitously, menacingly to the left, eventually leading to a clearing where an untouched sea of hauntingly fogbound evergreens stretches out as far as the eye can see. Caught unawares by this sudden clearing, I stop to gaze at the unsurpassed beauty.

I close my eyes and breathe deeply, as though I can inhale the fog and unmask the trees for the forest. But when I open them, the fog remains undisturbed. I take one last look deep into the unknown wild, searching for meaning, and continue on.

The depth of the forest, the hidden river and waterfalls, the gathered moss, the undulating terrain—more surprises lurking around every corner, surprises afforded by a new and shifting perspective.

When I return to Virginia from the trip, I visit Marcela, part of our agreement to check in on each other once a week while living apart. In the hollow home where she lives, I regale her with the story of the hike.

"And then, I heard this splashing," I say, trying to build suspense as I pull up a video on my phone.

She watches. "Are those ... otters?!"

"Yes!" There's an excitement in my voice that feels foreign. I swipe to a second video, hand her the phone, and watch her smile.

"It's the first time in a long time I can remember being ..." I start, before swallowing hard, unable to finish the sentence, as though the next word was criminal.

"Happy?" she asks.

I nod and begin to cry tears of remorse for experiencing—in her absence, without her—the first inkling of peace in more than a year, longer even.

While driving back to my apartment that evening, I think about the forest teeming with life, about visible and invisible mountains, about peering through the clouds and fog, about the certainty of the sun rising tomorrow. I think about marriage, with its uneven terrains.

I think about life and death. I think about the edge of that river, and falling leaves, and the melancholy moon. I think about shared moments with Dad, with he who painted my sky.

And in this shifting perspective, I recognize my error and finally begin to understand. The back-and-forth pacing wouldn't be the only hike he and I would ever share. No, I can find my dad's essence in every moment that brings me happiness, peace: his singing in the birdsong; his mystery and hard exterior and hidden emotions in the heavy fog and icy edges and black rock; his playfulness in the otters; his seriousness in the calm lake; his love of rain in the mist; his twinkle in the golden glow on the mountain's slope—his entire life, his entire being, captured in the ups and downs, the mountains and valleys, the light and dark. We would share not just this hike, then, but every hike until the day when our two suns rise no more.

The tears weren't of remorse, but of joy. And with this epiphany, the smile returns again. It's all about perspective.

Life is full of surprises indeed, Dad.

15. The Gospel of My Father

The hint of comprehension that my father's presence could be felt everywhere—still incomplete, unformed after the trip to Oregon—carries forward as late autumn turns to winter and I travel to Pennsylvania to sit with him. Though I often visited my father alone, a choice born from a desire to preserve the sanctity of our remaining time together, on this occasion, Marcela tagged along. Another visit home for Christmas, though one extrinsic to the memories of my youth.

This was the Christmas before the pandemic crippled the world, imposing limitations on my ability to sit with my father, watch over him, begin to make amends for the many years when I failed to give him my time. I am ashamed to admit the apathy I felt concerning these limitations.

It's a Thursday afternoon when I park the rental car behind this, his third nursing home, and turn the key in the ignition. The engine comes to a stop, and the car lurches forward as I let my foot off the brake too quickly. In silence, I sit—for a minute, maybe two, shielded by this metal-and-fiberglass cocoon from the outside world—from its smells, its noises, its ugliness and pain and heartbreak. But other thoughts and emotions absorb my attention, and this cocoon can't shield me from the communion between head and heart as I gird myself for another depressing visit sitting by his side, in silence.

I finally summon the resolve to open the door. Stepping out into the raw winter is like stepping from a soundproof booth into the unmuted reaches of my conscience. In the way speeding thoughts crisscross my neural pathways, the noise of cars crisscrossing the neighboring highway violates the erstwhile still silence. It occurs to me that these cars carry individuals living parallel lives—lives that, like mine, involve joy and sadness, happiness and heartbreak, hopes and fears. I think about the parallels and where these unknown lives are going in this moment.

Maybe it's a stay-at-home mom or dad, running errands before the school day ends. Perhaps she is occupied by thoughts of what to cook for dinner, whether he remembered to finish the last load of laundry, whether the kids will be better behaved tonight.

Or maybe it's a man in a rusting pickup truck, driving to the bank for a cashier's check to pay the rent. Perhaps he's occupied with fear of being unable to afford food and gas with the little left after he pays the rent and utilities because the factory where he works is laying off more workers.

Or maybe it's a family going to visit a sick grandparent in the hospital. Perhaps each is thinking, *Let's get this over with so we can get to dinner*, all of them reticent to voice the sentiment for fear of being thought uncouth, insensitive.

And maybe that's what I'm thinking as I briskly walk, and Marcela chases after, the hundred yards from the car to the building entrance. And maybe I'm also subconsciously hoping that, by arriving to the front entrance sooner, I can stave off the trepidation and reflection that might cause me to shamefully abort the visit, return to the still-warm car.

I breathe deeply, the brittle, bitter air warming in my nostrils. Inhale, exhale. The distinct sour smell of hospital food being cooked: the nursing home staff preparing dinner. Inhale, exhale. Cigarette smoke: a wheelchair-bound woman wrapped in a gray wool blanket, indifferent to the hazards associated with smoking while a clear tube wrapped behind and over her ear and under her nostrils ironically supplies her with the supplemental oxygen necessary to continue puffing. Her eyes meet mine. She looks at me with wistfulness, if not also resentment, as she puts the filter to her lips and takes another long, slow drag. I look at the ground.

Though my father's room is located on a secured first-floor ward, all visitors enter from the second. Crossing the threshold of the entrance is like stepping back in time. A waiting area where no one ever waits greets forlorn visitors. The open concept features cones of mellow lighting thrown against the walls by table lamps set on dark wood accent tables, gunmetal gray carpet with rug burn-inducing pile, and a tufted sofa upholstered in vertical striped fabric oddly reminiscent of a tightly spiraled candy cane. These features might be labeled "retro" or "vintage," but they strike me only as outmoded— less choice, more apathy.

As I adjust to the surroundings and tamper a growing sense of dread, I notice the gray-haired woman in her seventies seated behind the counter to the right. The pallid, inelastic skin drooping from her rotund face cannot conceal the heat foisted upon me from under sunken, scrutinizing eyes. Ignoring her impertinent stare, I sign in on the visitor log and grope for a visitor badge, distracted by pages concaved by the weight of countless heavy-handed visitors. Having secured a badge, I tell the curmudgeon thank you—for what, I'm not sure—and we walk to the elevator all while the sickening stench of subpar food intended for sustenance, not enjoyment, continues to nauseate.

Arriving at the metal coffin that will lower us into the bowels of this unholy crypt, I press the call button before remembering I must first enter a three-digit code, a safety feature designed to prevent internees, especially the high-risk dementia ones, from escaping. *What's the damn code?* I think, hard, searching my mind, before shamefully admitting to no one: *It's been so long since my last visit.* I send a text message to my brother.

"What's the code for the elevator at the nursing home?"

"5-4-3," he responds.

I press the code, and after a few seconds, the metal door reluctantly opens. *Once more unto the breach …*

While descending, I busy myself with the posted inspection certificate. *Last inspected three years ago? That doesn't seem safe.* I point it out to Marcela in search of levity.

The elevator creaks, the motor whirs and hums loudly, before the box stops at the bottom with disturbing abruptness. The wheels screech as they spin to mechanically draw open the heavy metal door. That the elevator functions at all leaves me feeling something like surprise; it does so only begrudgingly. Then again, perhaps that's my subconscious projecting.

When the door opens, we turn left into a sterile hallway illuminated by the unforgiving fluorescent tube lights. The hallway teems with activity. Nurses move back and forth, making notes, administering medications from their mobile carts, attending to the residents' myriad requests, balling up and burying soiled bedsheets in oversized laundry baskets, delivering meals and feeding helpless residents. It's thankless, their job.

For their part, the internees mill about. A few pace the hall; others sit and converse, watch the surrounding flurry of activity in the way one might sit on a porch on a cool summer evening watching passersby, or stare catatonically beyond the walls. One wheelchair-bound woman pulls herself along using the thick plastic railing affixed to the wall.

The noise is overwhelming. Nurses converse above the din, reviewing whether this internee ate, whether that internee was bathed, whether a date last night will lead to a second. They ignore the mumbling, screaming, and yelling, as though through experience they've developed an intuition, not unlike a mother with child, for when the yelling, screaming, and mumbling signals loneliness and wants rather than distress and needs. For my part, my internal screaming signals both the want and need for the silence of the car.

I walk down the center of the hall slower now so Marcela doesn't fall behind. Head up, eyes fixed squarely on a horizon of blueish-gray cinderblock walls, dodging residents and nurse carts and a fresh spill on the speckled beige-and-yellow tile floor. Straight down the hall, right at the Y formed at the intersection by the nurses' station, ten rooms down on the right. *Keep walking.* I shrink into myself, attempting to pass unnoticed, to avoid being drawn into conversation with an internee, a conversation that might only further prolong my visit.

Nothing can prepare me. No matter how many times I make this trip, no matter how many times I visit, each time I find myself woefully unprepared for what greets me when I enter my dad's room.

I find Dad consigned to the same position as when I last visited this "home," as though he's been preserved, suspended in amber. He appears the same physically, but I can still identify the deterioration. His wan, waxy skin drapes over brittle bones, resembling less a human and more a blob of tissue, atrophied muscle, and fat—though increasing less and less—like some Dalí Danny DeVito.

This threadbare body lies on the twin-size mattress, his knees slightly bent and askew; his back elevated, supported by an adjustable frame lowered close to the ground to prevent against severe injury should he roll off during his regular hibernation; his arms by his sides; his fingers rigidly curled as though rigor mortis wants the advantage of a head start; his hands periodically and involuntarily jerking; his skin cracking, flaking; his remaining silver-gray strands of hair strewn in every direction across his balding, spotted head; his mouth agape, lips pale and dry; his weighted eyelids closed to all light, not relaxed in peace but, rather, winced in discomfort.

We find not one but two folding chairs propped against the wall in the corner of the room. I place one bedside, by now a mechanical act, and Marcela places the other near the foot of his bed; an audible hiss escapes the vinyl padding when I sit, as though the chair sighs the years of pent-up weight, disappointment, and woe.

Since my dad no longer opens his eyes, he doesn't see me. But even if he did, he wouldn't recognize me. Truthfully, I can't remember the last time he could. At best, I can only remember the unending stream of visits, echoes across the years when I spent fifteen, twenty, thirty minutes seated in the padded metal chair by Dad's bed, my inattentive attention shifting between him and my phone and a blaring television and a clock on the wall, our wordless colloquy turning silent soliloquy. How, after watching the seconds stretch for days, I would stoop over him, whisper, "I love you, Dad," and lightly kiss his forehead before fleeing the room and his condition and my remorse. I chose to believe he heard me then, felt me then, if only to afford some promise of assuaging my guilt and shame.

On this occasion, though, and for unknown reasons, my gaze falls only on him, finding no distractions to occupy my mind. I numbly observe the rise and fall of his chest, the sole visible animation of Dad's continuing survival. I listen to his breathing, a raspy breath lying somewhere between the quiet, in-and-out breaths of functioning humans and full-blown snoring as muted sobs from the foot interpose in our exchange; hers are the only tears relinquished on that visit, or any. And as I linger there, watching over him as the clock watches over us, a new question surfaces: *Is this what becomes of us—disquietude that fills a quiet room; sobbing and stillness the pale substitutes for grief and forgiveness?*

And I ache.

Not for the man lying before me, but for the dad who once was. Because this man is a far cry from the strong, lively, loving father I remember from my youth. While my memory may be colored by the heartless hands of time, this much is certain: this man—this rotting mass of skin and bones and organs and fat and tissue—is *not* my father.

★★★

My father believed in God. On most Sundays growing up, this meant he'd drag me to our local church, an imposing stone structure built in the Gothic Revival style. And when the bronze bells pealed, signaling our magical transmutation from sinners to saints, I would take my seat at his right hand in the creaky wooden pews.

His insistence on attending was part of that Anglo-Saxon tradition of placing the onus for inculcating values on the church and religion. I suppose some of it stuck; some of it informed my beliefs and values, made me a better person, if only nominally so.

But I hated it.

I hated waking early on a Sunday and being forced to dress in khaki pants and a button-down shirt. "God doesn't care what I'm wearing," I assured Dad.

I hated sitting in a stuffy church in stuffy clothes singing stuffy hymns that made little sense to me, my father's stale coffee breath emanating as he monotoned along with the organ and other chanting adults.

I hated listening to the sermon, during which the pastor droned on in a similar monotone about adult things and adult problems—like healthy communication and marital discord—when all I wanted was to spend that hour focused on kid things and kid problems, like video games and responding "yes," "no," or "maybe" to a certain freckle-faced, auburn-haired goddess's note.

But my father believed in God, and therefore I believed in God, and so we went.

His faith trickled down economically in the letters he wrote me during boot camp. Letters that included frequent affirmations like, "Yes, I agree it's God's plan. He gives us the direction but we don't always follow his ways," or "I am with you all the time with my thoughts and prayers," or "I pray and ask him to watch over you and I'm positive he is doing that," or "As always, you are in my prayers—love you—miss you—take care—it won't be long now." And though my belief in God waxed and waned over the years, at times steadfastly Christian and at times dabbling atheist, I admit finding comfort in my dad's repeated prayers, his sturdy faith.

That's not to say he was a saint. My father took the Lord's name in vain, committed innumerable sins, and failed to live Jesus's teachings more days than not. But his faith Mondays through Saturdays matched that of Sundays. And, to my knowledge, my father never lost his faith in God, even when Alzheimer's gave him every reason to turn against Him.

My father demonstrated his faith most through nightly prayers. In my youth, I'd occasionally catch him sneaking into my bedroom late at night once he thought I had fallen asleep. I'd hear him turning the doorknob gingerly, maintaining tension on the contracting internal springs to keep from rousing me, before creeping barefoot to my bedside. With one pupil peeking from below a half-drawn eyelid, I'd observe him kneeling, silhouetted by the soft moonlight filtering through the cream-colored pocket curtains pulled tight against the night, his lips moving as he uttered his hushed prayer, the whistling whisper of his words unintelligible to anyone other than him and God.

Dad's prayers were short. Fifteen, thirty seconds. Just long enough to beseech God to watch over me, protect me, keep me healthy and safe. Once he finished his silent pleas, he would rise. Sometimes Dad would deposit a soft kiss on my forehead before exiting as quietly as he had entered. Other times he would steal a few precious seconds to watch me "sleep."

These episodes never felt creepy. Odd maybe, but in retrospect, touching—the secretive tender displays of a father's stirring love, undying devotion, and belief in a force beyond all force who might keep his family happy, healthy, and safe.

So much for that.

★★★

It's been a little more than thirteen years since doctors diagnosed my father with younger-onset Alzheimer's. My memory of that moment, the moment when I received confirmation of the presumed yet foul truth, seems inaccessible, cloaked in a waxy overcoat that protected me—then and now—from the descending tempest of emotions. Did the news arrive by way of text message or phone call? Was the exhale of "Alzheimer's" like the strike of a match that preceded the flame that was to devour all oxygen within the glass house I had built? Did my heart accelerate, did my palms sweat, did my body feel heavy—did I drop a single tear? The answers: lost to eternity under the weight of a whimpering slog of succeeding years. At any rate, he's lived far longer than I expected given the diagnosis.

I wish it weren't so.

I hate wishing for the end. I hate wishing for death to steal my father's final breath. It feels unnatural, this summoning of death for someone you love, admire, and respect. It feels unnatural, this eagerness for news that Dad has finally succumbed, that his brain has finally stopped giving the orders necessary to sustain the body's most basic functions, that all life has finally departed with one unremarkable exhalation. And yet, notwithstanding the impropriety of it all, a wish for my father's death routinely enters my mind, a path trodden repeatedly since the moment I last observed any resemblance to recognition in Dad's eyes.

Of course, there's so much to this that feels unnatural. Children aren't meant to lose their parents this soon. We're meant to learn and grow while our parents continue to pass along timeworn remedies for the unique hiccups that inevitably arise in adulthood. We're meant to establish careers, marry, build a family, all of which serve, in some way, as a form of time travel for our parents, vicarious glimpses into the past of a life well lived. We're meant to watch as our parents savor their hard-earned golden years.

Maybe this is idyllic. Maybe this is a storybook ending that has no basis in honest reality. Maybe this isn't "God's plan" or what's meant to be. But even so, that expectations so rarely meet reality does not make the pain or anguish or frustration any less real, any less valid, any less vivid. Because my father will have no golden years. Alzheimer's robbed him of that, the hard-earned fruits of his labor. And it robbed me of a father.

It's not supposed to be this way, so if this is "God's plan," if these are "His ways"—then fuck God.

Watching Alzheimer's slowly wreak havoc on my father's brain and body has caused me to think about death far more than I expected at this age. Whether it comes suddenly, unknowingly, randomly, or plods along endlessly until one's final breath, death arrives in many forms. But no matter the form, each death is tragic, presenting its own unique circumstances, hardships, profundity, grief, and loss. There is no "better" form of death.

But there's an ocean of difference between objective measurements and personal preferences, between the "better" and the "preferable." Does sudden death hasten pain, like ripping an adhesive bandage from the skin? Or, having been deprived of an opportunity to say goodbye, does the sting linger longer? Or is it a distinction without a difference? Death is death, and only just.

Though I've had the fortune to never suffer an unexpected death of a loved one, this experience with Alzheimer's draws me to the former, a preference for the quick over the plodding. Because, like many terminal ailments, Alzheimer's can be an excruciatingly lengthy death, one that follows two parallel yet uneven tracks. A torpid race where death plunders the nonmaterial, metaphysical, and spiritual conditions before snatching the body in one final covetous power grab. As Alzheimer's begins to increasingly and indiscriminately grip the brain, causing corporeal decay, it also begins to eat away at the host's existential characteristics.

This metamorphosis proceeds slowly with small changes to personality but rapidly increases as the condition progresses. And as the adhesive bandage is pulled centimeter by stinging centimeter from the skin and tangled hair beneath, the surrounding family watches as the person we know and love metabolizes into something new. A terminal illness of any kind is without doubt cruel, but my father's condition seemed unnecessarily so. Then again, maybe cruelty is measured in proximity.

I once attempted to convey to Marcela the experience of killing from a distance in combat. I explained how I'd watch the missiles strike their target and stare at the residue long after, in search of movement.

"It's not fun to watch someone die …" I started to confide. "There's no joy in watching another human die," as though death could—should?—ever approach the walls of joy.

From the corner of my eye, I could see Marcela staring, grimacing. I worried about her perception of me.

"It's not like the movies," I continued. "Bodies don't just fall flat. It's odd, sometimes. Like the body becomes frozen in death's grip. You'll watch a guy get struck, and when the smoke and dust clears, his legs will be contorted and his arm will be bent at the elbow and sort of raised toward the sky with the wrist dangling, frozen in that position."

More silence.

"Sometimes the body will twitch. The person is dead, but the body still twitches. Phantom twitches. It's like a lizard's tail wriggling after it's been cut off. Sometimes you'll see blood pooling. It's just ... awful."

But watching in painstaking slow motion the death of a *person*, unable to help, unable to intercede, unable to reverse the process; watching in painstaking slow motion as a loved one ceases to exist, not in a physical sense, though there is an element of that, but as an *individual*—that's a special kind of hell. And it's the special kind of hell the family experiences with Alzheimer's. A slow death, the "long goodbye."

The afflicted suffer tremendously, of course. One of the things that makes us human is our ability for higher cognitive function. The brain controls more than our biological functions; it controls our personalities, our emotions, and our thoughts. Alzheimer's attacks inner consciousness, the awareness of one's self, the capacity to recognize our own existence—the converse to Descartes's, "I think, therefore I am." How terrifying must it be to remain conscious of your brain rotting and being utterly powerless to halt the decay? How terrifying must it be to perceive the deterioration of what makes you human, what makes you *you*? And what about when all inner consciousness ceases, when you can no longer identify the *I*? In a literal sense, the afflicted observes through the mind's eye himself becoming less human, more animal.

At some point, though, the lines on the graph intersect. The afflicted's cognition disappears completely, losing consciousness of the *I*, the brain functioning only to sustain the most basic of bodily functions. But not so for the family. No, the family must continue to suffer. First, the memory loss. Then the changes to personality. Then the ability to recognize a spouse or children. And finally, the complete disappearance of the person we knew and loved. In this way, it seems, Alzheimer's imposes a suffering that reaches deep and wide, lingering far longer for the family than the host.

It's these thoughts, and others, that swirl as I watch Dad "sleep" in this unforgiving bed in this white cinder block room.

Here he lies. The man who chopped wood for hours using a heavy splitting maul; the man who effortlessly launched me like a missile from his shoulders in the pool; the man who took me bowling on the days when school closed for snow; the man who allowed me to score and solder glass shards destined for one of his stained-glass pieces; the man who offered advice on bullies, girls, and careers as we shared coffee on our covered front porch as thunder and lightning clapped and cracked around us—now reduced to little more than a shell of what once was, a vision of what could have been, a pitiful reminder of life's fragility, its transience.

And here I sit. Watching over him, standing vigil, praying. All of it—the aftershocks from my last deployment, his world-shattering diagnosis ten years earlier, the years of cascading effects and weary visits—brings about a certain distaste bordering on hatred for God. I am angry for all of it, but also, and perhaps above all, I'm angry because I can no longer enjoy these moments with a living father, can no longer solicit his advice, can no longer receive his hugs. I am angry at a divine, almighty being who could exhibit such cruel indifference, who could permit the premature deaths of innocents. Yet I continue to pray.

I wonder whether, in the aftermath of his diagnosis, my father shared my anger at God. Or did he continue with his faithful supplications until that invisible omniscient hand extinguished the flame of his all-too-brief candle? Did my dad remember then his declaration from eight years earlier, when he wrote, "It's hard to make you understand this but God has a way of showing us how to handle it"?

My prayers billow skyward with the rising smoke, filtering through the drab cotton curtains and casting a pale gloom over the room. Except, unlike my dad's prayers over me in childhood, I'm not praying for his health. I'm not praying that he makes it through his trials and tribulations. I'm not praying for his success.

I'm praying for a death, not a life. For a release, not an intercession. For an end, not a recovery.

I'm praying for the death of suffering—his and mine.

Even so, my heart is wrung by the thought of losing my father, my guiding light. But as the heaviness of this loss drags my heart across the rough washboard of life, squeezing the blood from its smooth fibers, leaving it limp to hang dry, I discover the unfathomableness, the foolishness of this thought. The truth was there all along, written by his hand. The gospel of my father.

His letters from 2000—the ones I saved, recovered, and cherished like talismans—took on an unexpected importance in a different "tough time," to borrow his words, helping to spark the long process of understanding everything that happened, everything I did (or didn't do) in Afghanistan.

But what I missed, and only now fully understand, is the other, and likely greater, importance to my father's letters: I am not alone in that long process. As he wrote then, "I am with you all the time with my thoughts and prayers."

So even when I lose him, I could never. His voice will continue to speak, not just through these written words but through the memories. My father's memory is—eternal.

This was the lesson in my father's sermon: even when I'm dead and gone, I will be alive in your heart, and you will be okay.

As I get ready to end this visit, I rest a hand on my father's wrinkled arm and lean in to kiss his blotchy forehead. "I love you, Dad," I whisper in his ear, hoping he can hear. "Goodbye, Dad."

And in an act of conversion, I repeat to myself the lesson of his sermon once more. *I will be okay, Dad.*

16. You Are Not Alone

In April 2021, an essay I wrote about the experience of serving as a legal advisor in a high-stakes, high-pressure combat environment appeared in *War on the Rocks*, a platform devoted to foreign policy and national security–related content. The essay was about me, but not. Not really.

After *War on the Rocks* agreed to publish the essay and I began working with the editor, my feet turned cold. *Does the essay really need to be so raw, so vulnerable? Once I relinquish control, am I prepared for what might come from exposing my demons? Could I handle the unavoidable negativity and ubiquitous trolling inherent to the anonymity and disconnectedness afforded by social media?* I struggled as fear and anxiety rose like the rising tide of the ocean: slowly, imperceptibly, until it was too late to step back and avoid the salty shame.

Notwithstanding my trepidation over the emotional consequences that accompany vulnerability, I needed to wrestle back control over the emotions tyrannizing my day-to-day existence. I had committed to this path. If baring my soul helped just one person, then standing naked in the public square was worth every painfully wrenched word.

I signed off on the final edits and waited. Whether I would walk with others or walk alone, walk I must.

The words began pouring in from all corners and walks of life, from unfamiliar faces and faceless names. Saturated with pain and relief, those words detailed shared experiences and the connectedness of the human condition.

The outpouring lifted my spirit. My essay had reached out through the readers' screens. Touching them. Grabbing them. Pulling at their heartstrings. Assigning words to the unspoken. In stripping bare, I had exposed my innermost struggles, allowing others to poke and prod and borrow that which felt intimately familiar.

A feeling of pride swelled with each positive message. Others had felt my words seep into their very being, as though, by discovering some secret passage to the stygian reaches of their souls, a place they had kept hidden from everyone including themselves, I had held up a looking glass through which they viewed their own broken reflections. In that moment, that frozen-frame of uncomfortable recognition, our souls connected in a uniquely human way. And I began to believe the essay had been a good thing, that putting it out there for all to see had given some hope to the hopelessly hopeless. My words had meant something.

But pride can be unwarranted, fleeting. And before long, I began to wonder if I had committed another betrayal. In writing the essay, I had exposed more than the starless night out of which no dawn arose. I had exposed the unbridled animalistic emotions of those with whom I served, the faultless but flawed emotions that had impregnated the decisions to abort another human life. I had exposed details about some of the innocent lives we unjustly though—as if it matters—unintentionally took. I had exposed the lies we told ourselves to absolve our consciences, to cling to our humanity while we paradoxically continued taking human life, after human life, after human life in furtherance of our mission. It seemed that the looking glass I had held up to the reader was just one in a dizzying house of mirrors.

Had I betrayed the organization? In exposing those private moments and dark shadows, in exposing our undeniable humanity, our occasional callousness, our tendency to err, had I betrayed more than the inner sanctum? Had I also betrayed my teammates' secrets, the secrets we keep even from ourselves? Did I have some moral obligation to remain silent, to remain morally straight in accord with our sacred creed? In being so honest, so open, had I failed to uphold our prestige, our honor?

My failures in Afghanistan represented betrayals of the beliefs and values that had formed my former identity. Was this essay, then, a second, separate betrayal, or was it a re-betrayal of those very same beliefs and values?

Or was this essay simply a belated attempt to reclaim that former self?

★★★

In the summer of 2021, and after living apart for nearly two years, Marcela and I moved into a new home in northern Virginia. Not long thereafter, we invited my brother and sister-in-law to visit for a weekend.

The invite, at least on my part, was, to a fair degree, selfish: I wanted to construct a built-in bookcase with a padded window bench in a spare bedroom, a project exceeding my elementary woodworking skills, and I needed Ray's help. After a four-hour drive south, they arrived with a truck bed full of tools, ready to contribute free labor and, as for my sister-in-law, Karen, worksite supervision and Statler and Waldorf-level heckling.

But my request was also something else. Reflecting on the times growing up when my father asked—or didn't bother asking, because he knew the answer—for my assistance around the house, or the many stories I had heard about my father and brother undertaking home improvement projects hanging new drywall or repairing crumbling chimneys, I felt pangs of regret and envy: envy at the time that father and eldest son spent together leaving tangible marks on this life; regret over not helping my father or learning practical skills from him when I still could, not spending enough time with him and my brother, and not prioritizing family over careerism. My awareness of these regrets arrived, like most regrets, too late for my father, but not for my brother. Mine, then, was an overdue attempt to recapture lost time.

We had just finished working for the day and joined our wives on the covered side porch. As the hot summer sun gave way to anonymous darkness, we sat relaxing in the reprieve, talking about everything and nothing, the familiar refrain of my most cherished relationships.

My father and I never spoke about his diagnosis. We didn't speak about life or death. We didn't speak about his fears and anxieties. Our normal changed—and would continue to change—before our eyes, yet we carried on as though nothing had, content to sip coffee as the circus pachyderm destroyed the room around us. But I always wondered if he and Ray had. And so I decided to ask my brother about this, about whether our father ever confessed any fears about his diagnosis and end of life.

I knew the conversation was one best had in person, so I held off on asking *the* question until we were together. But the right moment never seemed to arrive, and I procrastinated, putting off asking until "tomorrow." Now "tomorrow"—our last night together for the near future—had come almost without warning, and I couldn't find my voice. Even worse, when one stream of lighthearted conversation ended, another would begin.

I leaned forward in the rocking chair and began picking at the skin around my fingernails, present yet not, determined to outwait the conversation while searching the darkness for the beat when asking this somber question would seem natural in the surrounding score. Eventually the crescendo settled into a familiar stillness as we relaxed into the night, the world passing without notice. There would be no better opportunity, and I was running out of time.

I opened my mouth, my tongue pulling away with a click, and sucked in a breath, inflating my lungs, and courage. I held the breath at the top. *It's time.*

I exhaled, expecting to hear the sound of my voice, instead hearing only air passing through pursed lips. It was the sound of backpedaling. Asking the question would take more than one go, it seemed.

Once, twice more building the courage, but still only half committed. Consciously wanting to know the answer; subconsciously not. *Now or never, Eric.*

I broke the silence. My voice, which had developed a gravelly tenor at some point in the preceding three years, turned coarser still, cracking like a teenager expelling the first sounds of puberty, as though I was choking on the words scratching at my weakened heart.

"After Dad's diagnosis, did he ever talk about his fears? Was he afraid? Did you two ever have any conversation about the diagnosis and his thoughts about it all?" I mumbled, less a single question as originally planned and more a rambling series of thoughts touching on the same topic and strung together in meandering interrogatory form.

My brother sat on the steps at the opposite end of the porch and stared into the vinyl siding of the home (or rather, through the siding into the inside) his back propped against the post as he puffed from his cigar, his body a silhouette against the night. I watched the cherry glow brighter, casting a warm hue on his round face, before he pulled the nub from his lips and inspected it.

I could feel the air escape as my brother turned inward. He sat not twenty feet from me, but in that moment, it might as well have been twenty leagues. I turned away and stared into the umbra beyond, waiting for an answer I wasn't prepared to receive, for an answer beyond words.

"No, not really. I mean, he encouraged me to make amends with Mom, that she would always be my mom and that life was too short … He told me that he'd never stopped loving her … Things like that," Ray offered in a soft monotone as he continued staring through the siding. Another long pause, his gaze now turned on the cigar held between thumb and forefingers a few inches from his face. "I got the impression he was putting his affairs in order … That's how I'd describe it."

Things like that?! Putting his affairs in order?! What the fuck does that mean?! My brother's response raised more questions than answers. Was there something akin to fear or hesitation in Dad's voice? Or did his voice strike a note closer to uncomfortable resignation? Did it fracture under the strain? Was Dad's face contorted, depressed, relieved; his eyes weary, opaque, future-looking? Did he sob—oh, how there are few things as painful as seeing our parents cry—or did a single clear tear fall from the corner of his eye, roll down his cheek, magnify and reflect my brother's own fears? Did Dad try to hide his trepidation behind his clownish mask? Did Dad seem cold, distant? Did they embrace tightly, for a second or two or three longer than normal, the way one does in anticipation of a lengthy absence? Did Dad seem at peace with himself? The world? God?

I craved the details; I met repudiation. Something felt amiss. I had extended my hand in brotherly love, begging him to take it, yearning to connect with him. Instead, my brother gave me generalities and a minute, maybe less, of vulnerability.

After Ray and Karen retired for the evening, Marcela and I sat in the darkness as a light summer breeze pulled away the relentless heat. I had the nagging suspicion Ray withheld parts of the conversation with my father, that there was more he wasn't saying, but why the taciturnity? Was it that he didn't want to recount the details in the presence of our wives because those details were reserved for brothers alone? Was it that my question and the conversation it begged unearthed emotions he preferred to leave buried? Was it something else entirely, or was that truly the extent of their conversations?

I needed a second opinion, and I had no problem finding my voice now. Turning to Marcela, I begged her confirmation. "Is it me, or did Ray's answer seem cagey? Like there's more he wasn't telling me?"

"Yeah, it did. I think there's more there."

My brother's unsatisfying answer stayed with me for days as I worked through my own emotional stages.

There was anger, with Ray's refusal to share in the intimacy—that he'd deprive me of a deeper understanding of the man, my father.

There was envy, over the intimate conversation between father and eldest son—over the physical and emotional closeness that I perceived the two to share.

There was regret, about placing career over family—about rarely making time to visit, particularly after his diagnosis.

There was sadness, over my absence and the infinite loneliness my father must have felt—over the possibility that, as my father stared down the barrel at the end of life, he believed he had nowhere else to turn and resigned himself to suffering the tumult from within.

But then something broke the grip of reverie. And that something was a remembrance of the fortune bestowed upon me in the form of memories. I am awash in memories of moments shared, just Dad and I, doing unremarkable things, memories imprinted somewhere between birth and death on the parabolic curve of life. These memories form bits and pieces of my father—the intangible impression of his essence that I, and I alone, possess—an impression forever stamped on my heart. Alzheimer's could rob me of a father, but never Dad. In the end, that's all my father would have asked: that I hold on to the memories, that I never forget him.

It was nostalgia, then, that afforded me grace, compassion, and acceptance. My question had been an unfair one. I had asked my brother to relinquish one of two keys to a treasure chest of memories. He allowed me to peek through the keyhole, offering a glimpse of the contents but no more.

I cannot fault my brother for his reticence, for coveting the memory of this conversation—an unpleasant one, I suspect, but as one of the last intimate moments shared by father and son, no less meaningful in its historical place. I had no right to intrude upon that personal moment. My brother owns that memory, just as I own mine. These memories are all we have left: the timeless residue of our father.

In truth, the details were irrelevant. Like a rubbernecker, I sought only to satisfy my selfish curiosity. What I needed to know were not the details but whether my father discussed the diagnosis at all, a simple yea or nay that would reveal much about his mindset. On the one hand, if my father concealed the nagging thoughts that must surely accompany any terminal diagnosis, choosing to endure the rack through some veil of Victorian impassivity, then this would suggest not only an aversion to burdening others with his fears but also, and more rending to the heart, the absence of a trusted confidant. On the other hand, if my father openly discussed these nagging thoughts, then this would suggest he had someone to turn to, someone who held space for his feelings. Knowing my father, his truth likely lay somewhere struggling in the overlapping circles of both.

Even so, my brother kindly offered some conversational crumbs for me to devour, if only I could close my mind and open my heart. Because the secrets lay in his nondescript "putting affairs in order" and catch-all "things like that": my father had been reflecting on the long shadow of condensing time. He conceivably had examined a life lived, with all its delights and regrets, determined to remember the first and redeem the last before his fading brain failed both. None of this allowed time for lamenting his diagnosis. But even if it had, my father wouldn't have been keen on burdening others. My father focused instead on what mattered most for him, in obeyance of that all-too-familiar trope concerning life's transience, by making the most of what little remained in a rat race against the insuperable hands of time.

My father held the delights close, but redemption required something more. So my father entreated his eldest son to reconcile with the son's mother and confessed his undying love for her, his first wife, notwithstanding their tumultuous past. These small pieces paint a portrait of a man focused on the nuance of history, a man attempting to make amends, to right the wrongs, to atone for his past mistakes. One final lesson for his progeny in search of eternal peace for a restless soul. Maybe, as my dad had once assured me, God showed him how to handle it—that unambiguous *it*—after all.

Whether my father found atonement and peace remains the most aching of unanswered questions. I hope he did, before Alzheimer's looted that too. But that's one of many answers we can never have. Coming to grips with approaching death is, after all, a solitary process. We live much of our life in the shadows not of time but of mind and soul, alone with our thoughts and emotions. No one else can experience this for us or with us.

That my father spoke with my brother about anything at all brings me a not-so-insignificant measure of comfort. Because, while my father undoubtedly felt a degree of loneliness on his godforsaken march toward somber twilight, their conversation suggests the answer to one of my many heart-agonizing questions.

Dad knew he was surrounded by love; he knew—he was not alone.

★★★

I once again read the wounded words of readers who reached out in response to the *War on the Rocks* essay.

"Thank you for putting into words things that I have been trying to explain since I arrived back from my last deployment in 2019."

"Some of those quotes feel like they came straight out of my brain."

"I just read your article. It really resonated with me. It's so hard for people to understand being in that situation and how those decisions stay with you forever."

"I read your article first thing this morning. I cried. At my desk."

"I found your piece outstanding, and it spoke to me in a very direct/ personal way."

"[T]hank you for voicing what I'm sure too many of us feel but have difficulty admitting to or speaking out about."

"I connected to your words."

"[T]hanks for putting a lot of our thoughts and struggles out there."

"You put into words what all of us at some point felt and thought. [M]yself and others will benefit in knowing we're not alone."

"I felt compelled to tell you that your essay floored me—I've read it over a half dozen times. You were able to articulate the way I feel, and the way I suspect a lot of others feel as well."

"Wow. Okay. So … I've never read an article that so completely captures the immense stress and resulting weight of guilt from my personal deployment experiences[.] I'm not sure I can even put into words how validating this article is to read but also so completely difficult to face all of these feelings again in writing. It's a punch in the gut, but so necessary."

"I can't articulate properly the effect your article has on me, but it is profound."

"I didn't know how much I needed to read this one when I opened the article up."

"This made me cry."

And in those words, I discovered not some betrayal of an organization but rather a long-overdue display of intestinal fortitude. By admitting so openly the courage that had escaped me in Afghanistan, I had pulled it back from the edges. I had failed to speak in Afghanistan—to voice my objections, to push harder for investigations into recklessness, to demand accountability for entirely avoidable civilian deaths, to stomp and scream and shout to anyone who might listen and, when that failed, to do so with someone higher and higher and higher still—but not now.

This wasn't my intent, necessarily. I suppose that, in some meaningful way, I wrote the essay as my first act of repentance, a step toward finding the courage missing before. I hoped for mercy; I was prepared for judgment and ridicule, recognizing that judgment and ridicule might serve as my penance, one I was determined to bear with dignity.

But truthfully, I wrote the essay not for accolades, or recognition, or attention, or pity, or some confirmation of my so-called bravery or courage. I wrote the essay to witness my own betrayals and the resulting sucking chest wounds in the hope that I might serve as a vessel of vulnerability by which I could carry water for others—others who, I suspected, were concealing their soul scars behind an all-too-familiar public mask. I wanted to provide a voice to the silence. After all, I knew well the doubt, isolation, and loneliness that spurted from these wounds.

I wrote for them. So that they might find some solace, some warm embrace in my words, some atonement in my contrition; so that they might understand something my dad wrote me so long ago, something I hope he himself understood in the end: "You are not alone!"

Their touching words confirmed our mutual understanding. And with them, the clouds began to part. The sun shone brighter, the air felt lighter, the birds chirruped louder, the colors unmuted, the weight lifted, the throbbing chest dissipated, the smile returned.

Everything I needed was there, in Dad's letters.

Maybe this is what redemption feels like.

Epilogue

Dad,

I've written and rewritten this letter more than a dozen times now. In my head, in my heart, on paper. It's just that justice cannot be found in the constellatory combination of vowels and consonants formed over forty years. They dot the universe, beyond reach ...

I miss you.

The last few years—no, the last thirteen—have been hard, Dad. Really hard. Harder than I ever imagined anything could be.

It began, of course, with your diagnosis in 2008 and continues through the present. The intervening years passed quicker than many days, as though five thousand sunrises came to pass in a single night's slumber, and all the while a life beyond endured. I thought it best, then, to update you on the latest, just as you once did in letters to me at boot camp.

Rasputin is fifteen years old now. An ornery old dog, though that isn't new, he seems to have developed canine dementia, a twist of fate intended to compel recognition by keeping your condition at the foremost reaches of my consciousness. All the same, I feel a modicum of gratitude for this twist, which rouses happier memories of bringing him to visit you at that first nursing home, how you would lift him onto your lap and rub his ears.

Sasha, too, is older—fourteen years now—and is beginning to show her age. But she is the sweet to Rasputin's sour, a dog that models daily the importance of savoring life and all its pleasures in a way that reminds me of your thirst for living.

Then there's the newest addition, whom you've never met: Mishka. An Alaskan malamute, she dwarfs Rasputin and Sasha, though that doesn't keep her from enthusiastically attempting to engage both in play. Rasputin tolerates her, keeping to himself, and Sasha tries to ignore her—until Mishka charges at full speed, hurdling Sasha at the last moment and sending the latter into a thirty-pound fit of barking fury. It seems fitting the newest addition bears similarities to huskies since, from what I've been told, a husky was one of our family's earliest companions. While Kimba predated my time, the harmony between the different lifetimes and disparate circumstances warms me. And when I close my eyes, I can imagine Mishka's contentment under the touch of your gentle hand.

What more can I tell you beyond the dogs, who often provide the beams of sunlight on a string of overcast days?

You may recall Marcela and I holding a religious wedding ceremony in October of the year following your diagnosis. We had wanted an elaborate destination celebration, but your diagnosis and anticipated deterioration demanded a departure from those plans. As with many things in life, circumstances soon made the decision seem serendipitous: Marcela's father passed unexpectedly not a year later at the age of fifty-eight. It was a discomfiting parallel.

I met her father only once, at the wedding you attended; he lived abroad and Marcela had been closer with her mother. After walking Marcela down the aisle of the beautiful Roman Catholic Church not more than a block from our condo, he placed her hand in mine without hesitation or reservation. With a soft smile I had seen before and since in photos of him and eyes glistening with love and pride, a look I recall seeing reflected in your eyes on more than one occasion, he leaned into me and whispered, "Have fun." He was a good man, and though you two possessed unique personalities, you shared a certain vitality that most would consider infectious.

The effects of Alzheimer's were beginning to show that October. It hadn't robbed you of your clownish behavior, behavior displayed the night of the wedding while we—you and your two boys—danced on stage singing Neil Diamond's classic, "Sweet Caroline." A photo from that night catches us with mouths wide open, belting some line about times being good. You're wearing a polo shirt tucked into jeans, with shirt unbuttoned, as usual, exposing a tuft of silver chest hair, your olive Australian bush hat, I cannot explain. But you looked happy—exceedingly happy—and more often than not that's the way I remember you.

I experience many mixed emotions when I think about the days that bookend the wedding.

The night before, we held the rehearsal dinner at our favorite Italian pizza place. When the moment for traditional toasts arrived, Marcela's father stood to offer his well wishes. This was the first time our families communed, and he delivered his remarks with grace. Then, you stood. I think you were attempting to match his wisdom and words, an effort to again portray yourself in a way that would bring about the favorable impressions of others. But the disease, along with wine, foiled your efforts. As you fumbled over the words and thoughts, I felt my face flush as I looked to the father-in-law I had only just met with a pained look of apology. He smiled at me, attending to your remarks, and condition, with a kindness and mercy I regret not exhibiting, and I am ashamed now for my heartless display then.

Life continued uninterrupted as before: your condition worsened, my denial too.

That denial, deflected through distractions, soon led to the Army.

You know this, of course. And yet something about then stands out now as I pick through the disheveled remnants of life: for all the pushback you once gave me for various choices, you were surprisingly acquiescent in 2011 when I chose to leave the firm and enter the Army. I know now your memory and waning ability to grasp the meaning were likely to blame.

It was most certainly the reason I did not mention my first deployment when, a year later, our extended family gathered on the Outer Banks for Thanksgiving. At the time, the Outer Banks was recovering from the effects of Hurricane Sandy a month earlier. Though the storm passed offshore, it seemed to hover over the coast like a forecast of future deteriorating conditions.

I made the trip from Oklahoma to spend a few days with you before heading to Afghanistan the following month. I had intended to tell you about the deployment, but after arriving, I assessed little benefit from the revelation. Your short-term memory no longer appeared intact, you displayed erratic behavior, like removing your clothes in full view of family members or racing around like an out-of-control child in an amusement park; and your eyes held an unfamiliar hollowness. Yet you seemed joyous, as if blissfully ignorant of your decline. There was no need to tell you about the deployment, to deprive you of your enjoyment and ignorance, to induce panic and worry that might aggravate your condition, even if only temporarily, so I abandoned my plan.

I called you every week that deployment from a clamshell hangar skinned in PVC fabric, using one of the phones arranged on white plastic tables, while sitting on a folding metal chair, with only an inch-thick, two-foot-by-three-foot cubicle panel pledging privacy between our conversation and the next. Like visiting day at a prison if you replaced the orange jumpsuits with camouflage uniforms, shackles with shoulder holsters, and clear partitions with plywood sheets.

These were "morale calls," but that seemed an exaggeration, barely a euphemism. "You're there, and I'm here," it meant. I'm not sure whose morale those calls were meant to boost. It wasn't mine or yours.

For all you knew, I was calling from Oklahoma. It could've been from Pluto, and you wouldn't have known different, the connection would've been just as good too.

At first, I attempted to engage you in conversation. But the unnatural pause between the call and response, along with your abridged replies, told of this wild gambit, of the parallels to a conversation with a toddler.

"How's the weather, Dad?"

"Yeah ..."

"What did you eat today?"

"Uh-huh."

"How are the dogs?"

Uneasy chuckling.

And somewhere between your "yeahs," "uh-huhs," and inept laughter, and overhearing the neighboring conversations about children or finances or the longing of absence, my eavesdropping on our conversation became clear. I was participating in a soliloquy, left to imagine the response the way one does with the cell phone conversation of a person at the next table over—when I knew you were already gone.

You never knew about my deployments to Afghanistan, never had occasion to worry about me. For that, I am grateful.

My final deployment—that was the one, Dad, that changed everything for me, about me, the one that did me in.

I had enough sense to seek help soon after my return. For once I didn't care about my career. I was worried, scared. I wanted to find the old me.

Since then, I've tried cognitive behavioral therapy, acupuncture, running, yoga, massage therapy, and meditation. None of it seemed to help.

One treatment showed promise: stellate ganglion block. This procedure involves injecting a local anesthetic into a bundle of nerves located near the cervical vertebrae in an effort to reset the body's flight or fight response. After assessing the potential side effects, I decided I had little to lose.

On a bright and clean Monday morning, Marcela drove me two hours to the clinic. We arrived with enough time to enjoy coffee and conversation, both of which served as welcome distractions from the impending needle. I could still sense our anxieties rising.

Because of a global pandemic caused by an infectious disease outbreak, she could not observe the procedure. She walked me to the doctor's office where we hugged and kissed goodbye, nervous but hopeful—cautiously optimistic, even.

Then she left. Then they ushered me into the room. Then I was alone.

The room resembled most medical clinic rooms: a table lined with a disposable white paper sheet, a sterile white pillow, a wall lined by cream cabinetry made from medium-density fiberboard and overlaid with laminate, a stainless-steel tray displaying the necessary implements still wrapped in protective plastic, an ultrasound machine, and a large poster of a turquoise ocean reaching to an azure sky and harmless cotton clouds. Instrumental covers of pop songs combined with soft lighting worked to calm the patient.

I was the opposite of calm. Clammy hands, a heart attempting to breach its cage, and surely a glassy stare provided the clues as my brain registered the loneliness of both the procedure and an unknown prognosis.

When others sold me on trying stellate ganglion block, they sent videos showing gleaming post-procedure patients or describing the before and after as "night and day." But after the procedure, I felt nothing. No change, no improvement, no emotion.

That's not true, Dad. I felt something: disappointment. And that disappointment from our dashed hopes lingered over me, and Marcela, during the two-hour ride home and for several days thereafter.

My condition hasn't improved much, unfortunately. In some ways, it's worsened. I've discussed this with Mom and Ray. They've listened attentively, offered advice, and shown compassion, as you might expect. Yet I still feel a particular emptiness tormenting me. Not through any fault of theirs; they're here for me, as I hope I will be when time calls me to their side. It's just an unshaped emptiness created by your departure: a fatherless father-son talk.

I haven't given up yet, Dad. I see a psychotherapist weekly for eye movement desensitization and reprocessing therapy, which is slowly, though irregularly, helping me become more present and self-aware; I suppose this is some improvement. And I continue to explore other treatment options. But I'm tired. I'm tired of the weight I'm carrying above and buried below. It's the same exhaustion I observed in your eyes growing up, and I wonder if you felt the weariness too. I wonder if that weariness has finally left you.

And what of my marriage? Like most relationships, it's complicated, a sentiment I know you understand.

Our relationship survived that initial decade. We sleepwalked through it, day to day, month to month, year to year, all the while teetering on the edge as something close to resentment piled up for both. She spent the years in unspoken fear about my unhappiness, pulling me closer,

I spent the years in unacknowledged denial, pulling away. She once referred to Afghanistan as a "wake-up call" for our marriage. She wasn't wrong.

We haven't given up. We reconciled and recently started living together again. We attend therapy and strive to communicate more clearly, openly about everything—even the mistakes during our marriage I'm too ashamed to admit having made, though have. We seek to understand each other, and ourselves, better than we did years ago. And, for the most part these days, we're succeeding in our efforts. That's not to say we don't stumble and fall. Some days we do. But then we get back up—often with the other's hand—and try again. We try our best each day, fighting to find our way back.

My lingering problems from Afghanistan complicate matters, adding a wrinkle that would break even the best of marriages. I notice it most in her face, her eyes. She looks strangely older now, as though the depth of years, which would ordinarily form even layers across time, have compacted with the weight of a heavy snow. But she's beautiful still, in every way and in the most important ways. An exceedingly loving woman who possesses compassion, like you, and an ability to grant forgiveness even where such grace is unwarranted. She's a good person, and I couldn't be more thankful for her.

So, as I said, the last thirteen years have been hard, Dad. A depressing descension into waning twilight.

I miss you.

And I still need you.

Therein lies the brutal irony: the roles are now reversed. When you needed me most, I was absent; when I need you most, you are absent. And is this my penance? Is this some karmic retribution for my actions and inactions in Afghanistan, for my betrayals of self, and, above all, for my betrayal of you?

I think I'm begging for your forgiveness. For the reason that what you needed then is what I'm giving you now. Except the now lags too far behind the then.

Would I do it all again, Dad? Would I handle your diagnosis differently? Would I join the Army? Simple questions, with no simple answers.

And did I find it, you might ask: that thing out there I searched high and low to find? Not yet. But maybe I'm starting to.

Because, while much has transpired since your diagnosis, grieving your death hasn't. And though I continue to occupy myself with distractions as an agent of avoidance, maybe now—I am finally beginning to grieve.

"Thanks for sharing your feelings about how you realize. I'm very grateful and was wondering when you realized those things. I just hope you don't forget them again."

What I wrote to prompt these lines in return is unknown, the details buried beneath years of trash in a landfill of human creation. I have a good guess, though, and the hint to unearthing the meaning behind "those things" or "them" lies in the whole rather than the part.

I find these lines tangled up in your attempt to lift my spirits and strengthen my resolve in the face of a metastasizing homesickness, a reaction to the sweeping insuperable emotions I was experiencing that first summer away from home. It's easy to imagine I wrote you with an effusiveness I never voiced, a weepiness caused by nostalgia, resulting in maudlin expressions of gratitude. What I wrote, and to what you responded, was a tardy thanksgiving: an appreciation for all you had done for me through eighteen years of life.

It pains me to read those words, Dad. Because, notwithstanding your earnest hopes, I fear I did forget again. Life inserted itself between us. I became so wrapped up in my own life that I forgot to acknowledge yours. I carried on as though time touched only mine, as though, while I moved forward, your life remained frozen, awaiting the return of your prodigal son. There would always be time to show my appreciation.

Until there wasn't.

Of the many faces you wore, there's one I remember most vividly. That face, perhaps more than any, seemed to capture the underlying discordant spirit within you. Neither melancholic nor happy, it contained a clashing combination of pride, forlornness, hope, and grief one can only describe as wistfulness. But this face always contained an overarching heartsickness overlaid with a disenchantment of sorts.

And fear asks without wanting to know the answer whether I purchased this expression at the price of preoccupation, absentmindedness, and ungratefulness; whether this familiar expression represented a longing for the love and appreciation you felt I had unduly withheld from you. So I dredge my depths, searching for an example of a time since when I expressed to you an appreciation for you, hoping to calm the stirring silty guilt. Each time, I come up empty.

I'm sorry, Dad. Because, of the many regrets I've amassed in this life, none stings more than this.

For all the memories that remain, I wish I had spent more time with you, soaked you up and soaked you in, laughed with you, cried with you, created more. This heavy regret over the lifetime of squandered opportunities perdures. Though if I'm not careful, they will overshadow the most important lesson you ever imparted, the one I forgot: the importance of showing gratitude. I wish I had shown you more.

Thank you, Dad. Thank you for everything you did for me, everything you taught me, and everything your memory continues to teach me. My honest hope is that this book of memories—this eulogy to your love in all its imperfections—begins to atone for forgetting. If it's any consolation, I won't forget them again.

I know the time has come for your story to end. Before it does, however, I want to remind you of one last sentiment you expressed in letters to me two decades ago.

As you recall, I left for boot camp around the middle of June. I know my absence evoked a nostalgia that ripped at your seams: "Father's Day wasn't the same without you here, and it was difficult," you wrote.

I asked your second wife—my stepmother—to purchase a model train car and gift it to you in my name. We weren't fooling anyone; you knew she paid for the train, and I knew you knew she paid for the train. It didn't stop you from thanking me. "The gift ... was very nice and I really appreciate it. Please don't buy me gifts like that. I want you to spend the money on yourself. Don't misunderstand me I really liked the gift and I don't want to hurt your feeling but next time a card will be fine."

That wasn't the end. You concluded your thoughts on this subject with one additional sentence. It's this line that comforts me today, even under vastly different circumstances.

"What I'm really trying to say is that you just remembering me is all that I ask."

I grieve for the life you were denied, an end that draws nigh. But I celebrate the life you lived, a survivorship that draws on memories. These memories bind us indissolubly. And though the words here may end, the sentiments expressed do not. They will be forever held in my heart, where you abide.

There are no happy endings to this story, Dad. It won't be the same without you here. But it will be okay. Because, when I need you most, I will have your letters—I will have our memories.

After all, remembering you is all that you asked.

I think that's all I need.

I love you and miss you,

Drake

Acknowledgments

So much of the last few years—my role in Afghanistan, the attempts to reckon with the lingering phantoms of that experience, the belated grieving for my father, writing this book—has felt solitary. An incommensurable sensation of emptiness reflecting not some communal isolation but more some remote and unknown desolation of spirit. It's the sort of desolation one feels on the heels of hopelessness, an experience lived singularly in our minds as we narrate our own past, present, and future.

But as with those filling similar roles in deployed environments, as with those who suffer from lingering traumatic phantoms, as with those who grieve the loss of a loved one, I was never alone in writing what you read here. (Thank you for reading, by the way.)

Though a writer works behind closed doors—if not literally then at least metaphorically—many minds help to shape what appears once the door swings open. This book is no different. And I would be remiss in overlooking the many individuals who helped make this book what it is today.

I am grateful for the team at Warren Publishing, who recognized the value in this story even through the weeds of the initial manuscript and gave me the opportunity to tell it. This includes Mindy Kuhn, Amy Ashby, and Melissa Long. I owe an additional debt of gratitude to my editor, Tracy Crow, who encouraged me to open up and bring the reader closer; to my copy editor, Erika Nein, who served as a formidable last line of defense and helped address various weaknesses, making the manuscript infinitely better; and to Chris Kinsley for catching the errors that somehow survived countless revisions. The fault for any remaining errors you may find lies solely with me.

Thank you to Miladinka Milic, who created the amazing attention-grabbing cover design that perfectly encapsulates this book, and Lacey Cope and Susan Soldavin, who provided invaluable guidance for ensuring these words reached the widest possible audience.

I benefited from several friends who graciously offered their time in reading the initial manuscript. Their feedback provided not only renewed momentum but identified gaps in the story. I am especially grateful to Annie Bacon and Lisa Jakub. Annie's reminder to look for what exists beyond hope and to extend kindness to myself helped ground me throughout the editing process. I found her willingness to share deeply personal stories touching and a testament to the power of witnessing to unite the human experience. Beyond that, she's an amazing songwriter and musician with a voice like Stevie Nicks. Check her out: Annie Bacon & her OSHEN.

Lisa talked me off the ledge more than once using her trademark Canadian humor, and occasionally tough love, and reminded me of who worked for whom as we walked her cute, spunky dog. More than anything, I am grateful for her friendship. Lisa's advocacy for mental wellness and unsparing work with military veterans continues to inspire and humble. I encourage readers to check out her resources at Blue Mala and the nonprofit veterans organization, Mission Flexible.

Lieutenant Colonel (retired) Bill Edmonds continues to serve as a sounding board, and I am blessed to call him friend. His book *God Is Not Here* is a stirring testament to the many pressures experienced in lesser-known combat roles and how those roles can traumatically affect even the toughest of service members.

Thank you to Ryan Evans and Doyle Hodges for taking a gamble on an unknown writer and offering space on the *War on the Rocks* platform for a vulnerable personal essay about my experience as a legal advisor in combat. To all those who read "No Legal Objection, Per Se" and reached out to me, your words were touching in ways I cannot fully express.

That essay provided some renewed sense of purpose in a purposeless void. I hoped it might help others suffering in silence for whatever reason and from whatever cause. I found no bigger supporters of my writing than Major General Joseph Berger, Colonel Sean McGarry, and Colonel Keirsten Kennedy, and their encouragement to continue writing propels me forward. I am indeed one of the fortunate few.

I was honored to serve with the 75th Ranger Regiment, a unit comprised of some of the most intelligent and professional individuals in our armed forces. When I returned from Afghanistan in late 2018, I found compassionate support where I had expected mocking resistance. Those Rangers, who had all seen their share of direct combat and who shall remain nameless, rejected any notion that I had no right to feel what I felt and embraced rather than shunned me. From the bottom of my heart: thank you.

The list of individuals who deserve thanks goes on and on. To those not named here, please accept my sincerest apologies. I assure you that your influence on my life, and these pages, did not go unnoticed. Any omission here reveals nothing more than one man's faulty, inadequate memory.

Finally, but most importantly, the most heartfelt appreciation and gratitude for my close friends and family—the first for their patience and presence, the second for their love and support, and all for not giving up on me (yet). Your presence in my life is a true blessing.

To my family: I know reading this story was, at times, painful. But I hope somewhere between the lines and paragraphs, the words and punctuation, you noticed the love—not just the love I feel for Dad but the love I feel for you. You have each played a meaningful role in teaching me countless lessons about life, love, and all the virtues to which one can aspire. Your impacts—and they are many—are as lasting as Dad's, and they've made me who I am today. That this book focuses primarily on one individual should not detract from the immutable fact that I would be nothing without each of you.

I reserve special recognition for one member: Marcela. Marriage is hard enough as is, and I've given you many reasons to walk away. And yet you've stayed. I believe that says more about your character, your spirit, and your love than it does about my worth as a husband. I know challenges for us remain, but I am thankful to have you in my life as wife and friend.

And, for the record, you ~~still look like~~ look better than Denise Richards.

CPSIA information can be obtained
at www.ICGtesting.com
Printed in the USA
JSHW030633100323
38733JS00004B/14